WHAT ATTRACTS MEN TO THE SACRED LITURGY — AND WHY

Jesse Romero

What Attracts Men to the Sacred Liturgy — and Why

SOPHIA INSTITUTE PRESS
Manchester, New Hampshire

Cover by LUCAS Art & Design, Jenison, MI

Cover image: *High Tridentine Mass Prostějov 2023* by Novis-M (Wikimedia Commons)

Sophia Institute Press

Box 5284, Manchester, NH 03108

1-800-888-9344

www.SophiaInstitute.com

Sophia Institute Press is a registered trademark of Sophia Institute.

paperback ISBN 979-8-88911-338-6

ebook ISBN 979-8-88911-339-3

Library of Congress Control Number: 2024942544

First printing

I could attend Masses forever, and not be tired. It is not a mere form of words — it is a great action, the greatest action that can be on earth. It is not the invocation merely, but, if I dare use the word, the evocation of the Eternal. Here becomes present on the altar in flesh and blood, before whom angels bow and devils tremble.

St. Cardinal John Henry Newman

The death of Christ is an eternal act. We temporalize it; we spatialize it. Think of a great log that has been sawed in two. We see a number of circles on either side of that cut log.... That's the sacrifice of Christ. It runs through history, from the very beginning, when God made an animal skin for the first parents to hide their shame; it runs through all of the symbolic sacrifices of the Jews; and it runs up to Calvary and from Calvary on into heaven itself. In fact, it began with the Lamb: slain, as it were, from the beginning of the world.

Ven. Archbishop Fulton Sheen

CONTENTS

Appendices

Author's Preface

THIS BOOK IS A result of my personal and heartfelt reflections on my experiences as a Catholic, struggling to be faithful and obedient to Holy Mother Church. I would probably be classified as a neo-con; that's a term to describe conservative Catholics who discovered the Traditional Latin Mass (TLM) after growing up with the Novus Ordo Mass (NOM)—the Mass that has most often been celebrated in Catholic parishes since Vatican II in the 1960s. Even though I've always had a high view of tradition in all things except the Mass, I never used to know or appreciate what it meant in my Church. Why? Honestly, it never really occurred to me to ponder the fact that there was a Mass before Vatican II. I do remember seeing pictures of my First Holy Communion: I received on the tongue, on my knees, at an altar rail—and the tabernacle was in the center of the altar above me. I was born in 1961, so honestly, despite those pictures of my First Communion, I don't actually remember ever having gone to a TLM. As far as I can remember, I've gone to NOM parishes all my life.

And here's the problem: You really have to shop around before you can find a parish that celebrates the NOM with reverence and piety. How often are we actually able to find a place where the whole atmosphere and attitude in the church shows to us, with the timeless words of the Last Supper, that the Lord and Giver of Life is changing the bread and wine into the Body, Blood, Soul, and Divinity of our Lord Jesus Christ? This moment of Consecration is the sine qua non, that is, the defining and indispensable heart, of Catholicism. As I travel around the country to give lectures on the Catholic Faith, I am saddened to see with my very eyes the lack of uniformity from parish to parish, from diocese to diocese. This "diabolical disorientation" that is penetrating the sacred liturgy is a direct attack from the devil.[1] We know this because Scripture tells us that God is not the author of confusion but of peace (1 Cor. 14:33).

When I was ignorant about the details of the rubrics and prayers of the old sacred liturgy, I was actually in blissful ignorance. But now that I have found the TLM and know that I have seen the difference between reverence and irreverence that exists in our universal Church, I am a Catholic man who lives with a broken heart. All I want is the reverence that is befitting of God, the reverence we used to have before the modernists had their "coming-out party" at Vatican II. All I want is to be part of a parish where the Faith is lived well and where God is worshipped reverently. A place like that carries its own force of appeal and brings interior peace. It is difficult to have interior peace when, for example, you know that two of the three priests at your NOM parish helped to elect Joe Biden.

As we look back to what was happening during Vatican II, there are some pretty serious and troubling questions we have to ask. For example, why was Archbishop Bugnini, whom credible sources have identified as a Freemason, in charge of the revisions to the liturgy of the Holy Mass? The Freemasons, whom we will discuss in more detail in the first chapter, are a secret society composed

---

[1] Several years after Vatican II, on April 12, 1970, Sister Lucy warned of "a diabolical disorientation invading the world and misleading souls" (https://conciliovaticano.blogspot.com/2012/09/pope-john-xxiii-died-his-last-words-on.html).

of archenemies to the Catholic Church. Another question: Why did we have six men who were Protestants advising on the liturgical changes made after Vatican II? Most likely, the sad answer to that is that their advice was supposed to make our Holy Mass more amenable to their Protestant communities by making it more horizontal—more community centered, more like a happy meal gathering. Ultimately, the NOM appears to be a gateway either to Protestantism or to becoming a "none" (the nones are the group of people who have no religious affiliation or practice).

What did the changes of Vatican II result in? We'll look at statistics in more detail in chapter 2, but briefly, 75 percent of Catholics went to Holy Mass before Vatican II (1965); after Vatican II, only about 17 percent of Catholics regularly attend Holy Mass on Sundays. As Pope Paul VI said in 1972, the "smoke of Satan" has entered into the Catholic Church, and there has been an autodemolition of the Catholic Faith occurring since the time of Vatican II.

Strangely enough, despite the efforts to eradicate the old Mass, there is something about it that even mainstream talking heads can't quite get over. If, for example, even Whoopi Goldberg takes the time to praise Pope John XXIII and bash the Latin Mass … I'm just saying, maybe we can conclude from that fact alone that it must be the pure, holy, reverent worship of God.[2]

Thanks be to God for His mercy on me, a sinner; despite all this confusion and dissent since Vatican II, the Lord woke me up, and I had an interior conversion to the Lordship of Christ. This happened through the charismatic renewal and Life in the Spirit

---

[2] Stephen Kokx, "Why Is Whoopi Goldberg Praising Pope John XXIII and Bashing the Latin Mass?," *LifeSiteNews*, October 18, 2023, https://www.lifesitenews.com/blogs/why-is-whoopi-goldberg-praising-pope-john-xxiii-and-bashing-the-latin-mass/.

Seminars. My doctrinal formation was heavily drawn from Catholic Answers, from the works of Dr. Scott Hahn, Dr. Brant Pitre, and Dr. Michael Barber—and from Jeff Cavins's biblical theology courses, as well as from my MA coursework at the Franciscan University of Steubenville. Moreover, much of my catechetical formation came from Ven. Archbishop Fulton Sheen's *Life Is Worth Living* book and CDs and from Fr. John Corapi's intensive study of the *Catechism of the Catholic Church*. I thank God for putting all these people in my life. Because of them, I went from living the life of a poorly educated, lukewarm Catholic to being built up in the riches of our Church.

Ultimately, the Church belongs to our Lord Jesus Christ. The Church is His Bride. Supposedly, Pope John XXIII would pray a funny surrender prayer each night before he went to sleep: "Lord, it's Your Church—I'm going to bed!" And so, as we get into all the details of what has been lost in the "mainstream" Church, what continues to be disrespected in the setting aside of the old Mass, take it seriously, but don't let it get you down too much. I'll let St. Padre Pio have the last word: "Pray, hope, and don't worry. Worry is useless. God is merciful and will hear your prayer."

Now, before you get started with the rest of this book, take five minutes and look up a short film: *The Veil Removed*. Why did I spill so much ink on the topic of the sacred liturgy? This little production, supported by Scripture, the *Catechism*, and the teachings and writings of saints and mystics, says it all. In a few short minutes, it shows you in an absolutely beautiful way how the Mass brings together Heaven and earth, angels and saints—all of God's creation—to wonder at, to worship, and to partake in Jesus' sacrifice on the Cross. If you want to get fired up for why this matters, watch that video. It will tell you everything you need to know.

WHAT ATTRACTS MEN TO THE SACRED LITURGY — AND WHY

PART 1

CHAPTER 1

Establishing the Basics

What Is the Mass?

In one of his homilies, St. John Chrysostom said, "The Cross is a war memorial erected against the demons, a sword against sin, the sword with which Christ slew the serpent." Calvary is the rematch of the battle that we saw first in the Garden of Eden; it is the great moment when Satan is defeated, in another garden, by the Second Adam—the Adam who sheds His Blood for His Bride, the Church.

Let me explain. The Crucifixion of our Lord on Calvary threw a rock into the pond of history. The ripple effect of that rock on the water is the Mass, and that's how you and I come into contact with Christ on Calvary. The Blood of Jesus flows through time and space into eternity through the Mass. Calvary is like a power socket, a power outlet. At Mass, we plug into Calvary—actual Calvary—the power source that makes its effects present to us here and now. This is not a reenactment. This is the real thing, and we are actually right there on Calvary during the Mass. Receiving the Holy Eucharist, which is the fruit of Calvary, is like reaching back two thousand years and grabbing hold of the Cross and letting the blood of Jesus pour over you and wash you clean. When you walk out of Mass, you are walking down the slopes of Calvary. The Jesus of Calvary two thousand years ago and the Jesus in the

Holy Eucharist today are one and the same: Jesus Christ is the same yesterday, today, and forever. To understand the enormity of the Catholic Mass, you must understand that the heavenly liturgy and the earthly liturgy are one and the same.

There's an old negro or black spiritual that captures the action of the Mass: "Were You There When They Crucified My Lord." Each verse helps us meditate on one detail of Jesus' Passion: first His Crucifixion as a whole, then His being nailed to the Cross, then His being pierced in the side, and finally the darkness that covered the whole earth when He died. While the origins of the song are not known for sure, it most likely was sung by African slaves in America in the 1800s. The first printing of it was in 1899. It's unique in that even though it is a Protestant song, its details are so spot-on that it is the only spiritual included in the Catholic Liturgy of the Hours. It captures the essence of the Mass by bringing us right to the details of what's happening on and around the Cross of Jesus. When you attend Holy Mass, *you are there at Calvary*. Talk about active participation.[3]

Portals to Heaven and Hell

The Mass is Heaven on earth: It transports us to spiritual Jerusalem. In Genesis 28:10–22, Jacob dreamed of a ladder linking God's two realms. We'd probably call it a portal. Jacob's ladder is the name given to the stairway that appears in the dream of the angelic gateway that leads to Heaven from earth. Obviously, this kind of portal is a good thing, but exorcists also talk about portals; in their battles, these portals are entryways by which demons can get into

---

[3]   *Active participation* is a term used in the teachings of the Church to talk about how the congregation should be involved in the Sacrifice of the Mass. We'll talk more about this later, especially in chapter 4.

a person, a house, or any other object they begin to possess. To combat this entry to demonic evil, and in fulfillment of Jacob's dream in the Old Testament, the Catholic Mass is also a portal. It is the entryway and ladder that God has ordained whereby angels bring sanctifying grace to a person's soul, and our prayers are taken back up to God by angels. St. Rose of Lima said it simply: "Apart from the cross there is no ladder by which we may get to Heaven." It is in the Mass that we find this Cross most directly.

For further meditation on this idea of the Mass as the portal between Heaven and earth, I recommend that every Catholic watch the movie *El Gran Milagro*, which was made in 2011. Its title in English is *The Greatest Miracle*, and it was produced in Mexico by Dos Corazones Films (Two Hearts Films). Although it is animated and so might seem simplistic, it is actually a great tool for individuals and families to learn about the theology of the Mass and all of the graces and unseen angels present with us in our participation at Mass. The Most Rev. David L. Ricken, bishop of the Diocese of Green Bay, said of this film: "*The Greatest Miracle* draws the viewer into the Mass by artistically portraying what we as Catholics believe to be taking place, but what we as human beings are incapable of perceiving with our earthly senses. It beautifully depicts the moment of the Consecration as a continuation of Christ's sacrifice on Calvary, and it celebrates the way in which we '… unite ourselves with the heavenly liturgy and anticipate eternal life, when God will be all in all' (*CCC*, 1326)."[4] Anyone who watches this movie will never see or experience Mass the same way again.

The Catholic Mass is the oldest construct in western civilization. There is nothing like it. Although it seems plain and

---

[4]   Lisa Hendey, "*The Greatest Miracle* Hits Theaters This Weekend," Catholic Mom, December 7, 2011, https://www.catholicmom.com/articles/2011/12/07/the-greatest-miracle-hits-theaters-this-weekend.

ordinary, there is actually an entire world that you do not see when the priest says the words of Consecration and raises the Holy Eucharist into the air. All of Heaven opens up and surrounds us at that moment, no matter what Church you are in. If God would allow us to see what happens at the Catholic Mass at the consecration, we would all faint with joy and happiness. Literally, Heaven comes down to earth, and we are surrounded by saints and angel's (cf. Rev 4:4; 7:9–17).

Words and Their Meanings

St. Thomas Aquinas liked to start his arguments by defining his terms. Taking a page out of his book, let's talk for a minute about some of the key words and phrases that we'll use in the rest of this book. First, a fun fact: Did you know that our word *Christmas* comes from an early English phrase, *Cristes Maesse*, dating back to 1038? Surprisingly, it doesn't mean anything specifically about the Nativity of our Lord. It simply means "Mass of Christ."

Now, down to business!

Novus Ordo Missae means the "New Order of the Mass," and it refers to the Mass that was given to us by Pope Paul VI in the 1960s through the machinations of Vatican II. As I speak about the two forms of the Mass in the Roman Rite, I will use the abbreviation *NOM* to refer to the *Novus Ordo Missae*. I will use the abbreviation *TLM* to designate the Traditional Latin Mass, which was celebrated for centuries before Vatican II.

Your first questions from here might be, How should we talk about the way we approach the Mass, and is there any precedent one way or the other? Do we pray it, offer it, read it, or celebrate it? In the TLM — that is, the Mass that was most widely offered from the 1500s until the 1960s and Vatican II — the priest generally says that we "pray the Mass." In the NOM — the Mass that we see most frequently today and that grew out of Vatican II — the priest says we "celebrate the Mass." Ven. Archbishop Fulton Sheen would say "read the Mass." However, many priests across the board say we "offer the Mass" because it highlights the sacrificial nature in both forms of the Roman Rite — that is, in both the TLM and the NOM.

Although traditionalists who might be dismissive of NOM terminology might not be on board with talk of "celebrating" the Mass, you might be surprised to learn that this is actually the oldest expression of the bunch. There is a very old prayer in Latin, the *Ego Volo*, that a priest prays in the sacristy before he enters the sanctuary to offer the Mass. It reads: *Ego volo celebrare Missam*, which means "I want to celebrate the Mass." While this specific prayer was written by St. Cyprian of Carthage in the third century, St. Thomas Aquinas in the thirteenth century and again St. Pius V in the sixteenth century also used the Latin *celebrare* in reference to the offering or praying of the Mass.[5] Little language trivia like this can help us remember, as we get into some of the more difficult differences in the following pages, the roots we have in common, no matter the form of the Roman Rite that we are used to.

Within the Roman Rite, Pope Benedict XVI gave us terminology to distinguish between the older TLM and the newer NOM. He called them the Extraordinary Form and the Ordinary Form. Within the Extraordinary Form, or TLM, there is a uniformity of actions, a clear role between priest and laity, a clear distinction between the sanctuary and the nave, and there is reverence, piety, and sacred silence. We will talk more about the atmosphere of the

[5]   Fr. Tim Finigan, "'Celebration' and the Pitfalls of Language," *The Hermeneutic of Continuity*, February 27, 2019, https://the-hermeneutic-of-continuity. blogspot.com/2019/02/celebration-and-pitfalls-of-language.html.

Mass, and especially the reverence and piety of it, in chapter 4. I would like to draw attention to the definition of the word *extra*.[6] As an adjective, it means "beyond or more than what is usual; larger or better than what is usual." As a noun, it means "something extra or additional; something of superior quality." As an adverb, it means "beyond the ordinary degree; done extra well; extra large." And finally, *extraordinary* is defined as "beyond ordinary, beyond regular, exceptional, remarkable, phenomenal, special," whereas *ordinary* is defined as "commonplace or average condition, something regular, customary, or usual."

What is technically meant here is that the Ordinary form of the Mass is given as the usual, customary form, while the Extraordinary form is additional or beyond what is usual. But it is worth noting here that these two forms of the Mass are not the only things distinguished in this way; exorcists refer to demonic temptations, which all of us experience on a regular basis, as *ordinary* demonic activity, but they refer to demonic possession, which is far more unusual, as *extraordinary* demonic activity. In other words, demonic possession is demonic activity that is operating at a much higher degree, one might even say a much greater and superior degree, than what is normal. When we look at this reverse example in the light of Benedict's terminology for the Mass, we can't help but draw out the implication from this that *Extraordinary Form* indicates the superior quality of the TLM based on the very definition of the word *extra*. While the NOM, the *Ordinary Form*, can be a beautiful Mass when celebrated properly, I would use the words of St. Paul to describe the TLM: "And I will show you a still more excellent way" (1 Cor. 12:31).

---

[6] The following definitions are from dictionary.com.

The Latin Language: Why Does It Matter?

So far, our discussion of language has been focused on how we talk about the Mass in our own language. But what about the fact that the TLM is, by definition, primarily in Latin? What's the point of that? For one thing, there's an advantage to using a "dead language" such as Latin for the worship of God. Because the meanings of the words in a dead language don't change over time, it is a lot more precise and constant in what it says. By contrast, living languages like, Spanish and English, evolve, which means that the meanings of words change over time. For one easy example of this that has a lot of impact on the world we live in today, take a look back at the lyrics from the original *Flintstones* theme song, written in the 1960s:

> When you're with the Flintstones
> …
> We'll have a **gay** old time!

Today, of course, the word *gay* is used in the English language almost exclusively to mean *homosexual*. In a more sacred context, think about this simple translation of Scripture from St. Paul. In 2 Corinthians 11:25, he says, "Once I was stoned." How would a twenty-first-century woke-college liberal pothead interpret these words today?

Spanish words evolve as well. For example, today Hispanic men generally call other men who are their friends or are men they respect *mi perro*, which means "my dog." If you had called a fellow Hispanic man a dog some years ago, you would have been asking for a fistfight. In the Old Testament, if you were called "a dog," that meant you were a sexual degenerate.

It is easy for us to see, then, that by contrast, a large part of the beauty and power of Latin is the precision of its words—words that meant the same in the fourth and fifth centuries (when the earliest forms of the Traditional Latin Mass originated) as they do today. But many theologians, and especially exorcists, have also attested to the power that Latin has over demonic forces. When demons hear the Latin prayers, they recognize it as "courtroom language." They know it has the authority of the Church behind it, and they are rightly terrified of it. Fr. Peter Carota tells us: "When Latin was removed from prayers in the 60s, all hell broke loose throughout the world," and he further says, "Latin Mass, Latin exorcism, Latin sacraments crush the devil."[7]

Noted exorcist Fr. Chad Ripperger also speaks on the sacred languages: "Actually, Hebrew, Greek and Latin were affixed to the instrument of our salvation (cf. John 19:19–20); that's why they're sacred. The Latin Mass was prayed around the world for centuries—this was the answer to the tower of Babel."[8] Where the confusion at Babel divided the world, the unifying power of Latin as *the* language of the Church provides an avenue for unity. If each Catholic Mass is said instead in the language common to each country around the world, wherever it is said, that unifying power is lost.

Latin is the official language of the Church and is an immutable, theologically tight language. It was the language used in all exorcisms until recently precisely because it is not a living language—and that means that the truth of its meaning is unchanging. Thus, it is a powerful weapon against the diabolical, since the ethereal (i.e., heavenly and celestial) spiritual battles are battles of truth.

---

[7]   "Why Pray in Latin?," *Praying Latin*, www.prayinglatin.com/why-pray-in-latin/.

[8]   "Fr. Chad Ripperger and Dr. Taylor Marshall Talk about Latin Mass, Latin, Exorcisms, Books, Prayer," *Taylor Marshall Show*, https://taylormarshall.com/2021/04/675-fr-chad-ripperger-dr-taylor-marshall-talk-latin-mass-latin-exorcisms-books-prayer-podcast.html.

Demons and the Latin Mass

A possessed man I know, a man who has gone through twelve sessions of exorcism with his diocesan priest, told me that part of his healing is gauged by how long he can sit at Holy Mass before the demon reacts with aversion, manifests through his body, and begins tormenting him. He said he can sit in the NOM until the Consecration, and at that point the demon will start to rage within him. But he said that the demon manifests and torments him in the Latin Mass as soon as Father ascends the sanctuary and starts his opening prayer. The demon recognizes the power of the Latin prayers and the reverence that comes along in that whole atmosphere, all of which works together to bring forth an avalanche of graces almost immediately. And the demons cannot bear such goodness, beauty, and truth spoken by the priest of the Most High God.

They have their own demonic response, of course. The devil himself knows that the true and purest form of worship to God on earth is the Catholic Mass, and so he has led his followers on earth into the atrocity that is a black mass, which is a demonic mockery and reversal of the Holy Catholic Mass. Satan tries to ape God, tries to set himself up like God, and tries to make his followers worship him in a gross and backward reflection of the beautiful and most perfect worship of God on earth. We know, though, that Satan can never win in his pathetic and blasphemous imitations. Scripture even tells us that Satan is *like* a lion (1 Pet. 5:8), but it also says that Jesus *is the* Lion (Rev. 5:5)!

One last thought to take with you if you wonder about how much demons hate the Mass: Kyle Clement, who is a case manager for Fr. Ripperger in his exorcism work, shared some of what they witnessed in a man from Denver, Colorado, who had been possessed. They observed that after simply reading a book about the Mass — Ven. Archbishop Fulton Sheen's *Calvary and the Mass* — this man was completely liberated from demonic possession. What a powerful gift we have in the Mass!

The TLM: Part of the Tradition of the Church

I mentioned earlier that the TLM has its roots in the third and fourth centuries. Since that time, the Latin language has been the home of the liturgy of many of the Church Fathers and the Doctors of the Church, from the Middle Ages to the Renaissance, from the Romanesque era to the Gothic and the Baroque, and so on until today:

> Many Saints have commented on their love for the Latin language and prayed both publicly and privately in this *lingua sacra*. The most famous Saints, including St. Augustine, St. Ambrose, St. Benedict, St. Patrick, Pope St. Gregory the Great, St. Thomas Aquinas, St. Dominic, St. Francis of Assisi, St. Anthony of Padua, St. Padre Pio, St. John Vianney, St. Frances de Sales, St. Alphonsus Liguori, St. Catherine of Sienna, and countless Saints throughout all ages of the Church all prayed in the same sacred Latin language.[9]

In his commentary both on the Latin language and on the changes brought about by Vatican II — and specifically on the loss of what had been the Mass of so many ages before — Dr. Dietrich von Hildebrand writes: "I emphatically do not wish to be understood as regretting that the Constitution has permitted the vernacular to complement the Latin. What I deplore is that the new mass is

---

[9]   "Why Pray in Latin?"

replacing the Latin Mass, that the old liturgy is being recklessly scrapped, and denied to most of the People of God."[10]

The first Mass, the archetype of all Masses, was consummated at Calvary—in the Latin language, as the Roman soldiers, who were the ministers of that Mass, went about their grueling business, albeit not knowing what they did. By the time it was over, some of these Roman soldiers believed and professed their faith in Latin (Mark 15:39) while others did not. And the Jews watched it all unfold. Some of them understood the Romans' Latin language well while others understood it only dimly or not at all. Some of the Jews believed (Luke 23:42) while others did not. And today, we, the Catholic Church, the "New Israel," now watch again, some of us comprehending the Latin while others do not, some believing while others do not (John 6:66–69).[11]

A Weighty Rivalry: Freemasonry and the TLM

Before we wrap up this chapter, we do, unfortunately, need to spend a little time talking about the conflict within and outside the Church that sidelined the TLM in the 1960s and that continues to try to keep it on the sidelines today.

The TLM has seen exponential growth during the 2010s and today, but for some reason, there's a lot of opposition to it, especially high up in the Church. Does that make any sense? Young and large Catholic families are filling the pews and standing and kneeling on the floor behind them because these Masses are usually filled to overflowing—and surveys show that these

---

[10] Dietrich von Hildebrand, "The Case for the Latin Mass," *Triumph*, October 1966, https://unavocecanada.org/wp-content/uploads/2016/01/Dietrich-Von-Hildebrand-The-Case-For-The-Latin-Mass.pdf.

[11] "Welcome," *Usus Antiquior*, https://propria.org.

Catholics are unusually generous in their parish contributions too. TLM religious orders are expanding, raising funds for new buildings because they are running out of space for all their new vocations—in convents, monasteries, and seminaries. TLM Catholics are also more likely than NOM Catholics to live by what the Church teaches when it comes to marriage, family, and sexuality. Whose idea was it to build up dislike against these faithful Catholics? It doesn't *seem* to make any sense, especially when you realize that they are being persecuted from within the Church herself. But it *does* actually make sense, and that is for one reason: the Freemasonic infiltration of the Church. The Freemasons are demonic, which means they want our damnation. So who are they going to attack? The Catholics who most closely follow the teachings of the Church, of course. If they can get every TLM parish shut down, they'll have a much easier time getting us all into Hell.

And don't think Satan's army of Freemasons is going to stop there. They know that whether it's a TLM or a NOM, the Mass is the most pleasing form of worship on this earth. They want to knock it out anywhere they can, to end the strong supernatural graces that flow from such a powerful form of worship. Because the TLM is the Extraordinary Form, the graces that come from it are also literally extraordinary. Freemasonry wants to hit at the most vibrant font of graces in its quest to eliminate the true worship of God; the TLM is the ultimate threat against it. In a letter to the Italian people on December 8, 1892, Pope Leo XIII warned: "Let us remember that Christianity and Freemasonry are essentially incompatible, to such an extent, that to become united with one means being divorced from the other. Let us, therefore, expose Freemasonry as the enemy of God, of the Church and of our Motherland."[12]

We've talked about all the awful cultural things that happened in the 1960s and 1970s and in the years since then that have had terrible effects on the Church, but we need to be honest with ourselves too. Think about it. Is it possible that, in the years since Vatican II, we ourselves have put a choke hold on the most powerful river of grace, strangling our Church from within? This is not some fringe conspiracy theory. Mary herself is the one who told us that Freemasonry would infiltrate the Church; this, in large part, is why, over the course of the twentieth century, we started to wither from within. As we already said, Freemasonry seeks to eliminate supernatural grace from entering the world, and the TLM is the prime target. Think about how much Rome has limited the TLM. If you want to know where the Freemasons are within the Church, look at the attack on the extraordinary avenues of grace in the TLM.[13]

Beyond the fact that Freemasonry seeks to destroy the Mass because Freemasons are agents of the devil, why else do they specifically hate it? Remember that first and foremost, the Mass is the sacrifice of Jesus on Calvary. It is the most pure and holy sacrifice that ever was. When we look back to Genesis, we see for the first time the difference between a righteous sacrifice and one that was not acceptable to God. The brothers Abel and Cain both worshipped God, but God accepted only Abel's offering, for he made his blood sacrifice with a pure heart. Cain did not offer a blood sacrifice, and he had an evil heart. The first recorded murder

[12] Paolo Reyes, "The Church Under Attack," *Totus Tuus, Maria*, http://www.all-about-the-virgin-mary.com/freemasonry-in-the-church.html.

[13] The Elder, "Freemasonry and the Traditional Latin Mass," *The Bellowing Ox* 10, no. 3 (May–June 2022): 11, https://kcrd-fm.org/the-bellowing-ox.

occurred because one brother was jealous of the other brother's worship being received by God. Catholic worship done properly is like the sacrifice of Abel. Those with the spirit of Cain (i.e., those who serve in Islamist, satanic, occultist, secularist, Marxist — and Masonic — legions) hate the Catholic Mass.

The Wolves Are Guarding the Henhouse

Unfortunately, before, during, and after the Council, the Church had been infiltrated by these Freemasons, and by communists and homosexuals. The zeitgeist — the German term for "spirit of the age" — was largely responsible for the decline in certain key aspects of the Catholic Church in the United States. We saw this decline in the number of priests and religious, in weekly church attendance, and in the state of Catholic marriage. The zeitgeist also fostered the rise of dissident Catholic organizations and individuals who have taught "the spirit of Vatican II" (i.e., erroneously formulated applications of the New Order of the Mass that have no real basis in text) in order to promote their own modernist agenda. It has not been difficult to promote this "spirit" since many of the documents of Vatican II were written ambiguously. According to Fr. Edward Schillebeeckx, a Vatican II peritus (the periti are the theological advisors for ecumenical councils), "we used ambiguous phrases during the Second Vatican Council and we know how we will interpret them afterwards."[14] In the face of such disastrous methods, "Pope Benedict XVI has emphasized the *continuity* of the Catholic tradition, insisting that the teachings of Vatican II must be interpreted in light of the constant

---

[14] Cited in Marcel Lefebvre, *Open Letter to Confused Catholics* (Kansas City: Angelus Press, 1992), 106.

teachings of the Church in the preceding centuries."[15] But very few theologians have listened to his insistence.

What does this mean for the future of the TLM? Cardinal Wilton Gregory of Washington, D.C., said, "Tradition dies a slow death, sometimes a bloody death," pointing out that "two hundred years after Trent, there were still places that were celebrating the pre-Trenten Mass, so it took that long." And, when speaking as to why the Ordinary Form of the Mass should be the dominant one in the Roman Rite, Gregory simply said that it's "because that's the Church's liturgy.... If you want to belong to another ritual family, you can be Ruthenian, you can be Maronite, you can be Melkite, but the Roman rite has one dominant rite." He added that the Church's goal is to unite people around the new Mass over time, also restricting the number of priests who are allowed to celebrate the old Mass.[16]

As one commentator has asked already, why is it that, in a Church that claims to want to encourage a diversity of cultural expression, the Extraordinary Form of the Mass, celebrated for centuries, is being marginalized — despite the good that it is obviously accomplishing wherever it is allowed to grow?

---

[15] "The *Motu Proprio*: Why It Was Needed," *Catholic World News* News Features, Catholic Culture, September 13, 2007, .

[16] Peter Pinedo, "Washington Archbishop Addresses Decision to Limit Traditional Latin Mass," *Catholic News Agency*, December 8, 2023, https://www.catholicnewsagency.com/news/256228/washington-archbishop-addresses-decision-to-limit-traditional-latin-mass.

CHAPTER 2

THE 1960s: THE SMOKE OF SATAN IN THE VATICAN AND IN AMERICAN CITIES

The Effect of the 1960s on the Catholic Church

THE 1960s WERE A horrible time for American society and culture. We experienced a social upheaval in the secular world—and of course Vatican II was going on during this time of turmoil. The devil never sleeps, but, boy oh boy, was he active in the 1960s. All of these occurrences were the catalyst for a new world order. Although this is by no means a complete list of travesties, here are some "highlights" from that time.

In 1961, secular humanistic hedonism gained a foothold in *Torcaso v. Watkins* when the Supreme Court ruled that those who hold public office no longer need to believe in God. This was followed by prayer being banned in public schools in 1962, Bible teachings being banned in them in 1963, the free speech movement (also known as the "filthy speech movement") being launched at Berkeley in 1964, and birth control being legalized by the Supreme Court in 1965. That same year also saw the founding of *Penthouse*, a magazine dedicated to erotica and pornography. In 1966, the "Church of Satan" was founded by Anton LaVey, in 1967 Catholic universities (Notre Dame chief among them) broke with the Church in order to receive federal funding and support — with so many strings attached — and in 1968 restrictions on the filmmaking industry that had previously maintained certain moral standards in movies were removed, opening the path to pornography. Building on Anton LaVey's work, the Satanic Bible was published in 1969 — the same year that the gay rights movement was started in Greenwich Village and the same year that the Woodstock Festival with all its atrocities happened in Upstate New York. People who witnessed the aftermath of Woodstock reported that, at the end of the four days of bacchanalia, the ground was covered in empty alcohol bottles, drug paraphernalia, cigarette butts, used condoms, urine, vomit, fecal matter, amniotic fluid and even placentas, blood, trash — and three dead bodies. This horrific decade was brought to a close with the first gay pride parade in Los Angeles in 1970, an event that saw participants dragging a twenty-foot papier-mâché penis through the streets.

In addition to these more specific events, let us not forget that we had the Vietnam War, the unrest and violence of the civil rights movement, the assassination of Rev. Martin Luther King Jr., and the assassination of President John F. Kennedy, who was (nominally) our first Catholic president. Against this alarming backdrop, in the midst of such a social milieu, Vatican II was convened.

The modernists in the Church were undoubtedly influenced by this mess of Western culture at large. This new world order, called "the culture of death" by Pope St. John Paul II, put modernism and liberalism on the fast track in the Catholic Church. Even the name of the Mass was changed in a reflection of the new flavor of the times: the "New Order Mass." This is why Archbishop Viganò wrote: "In reality, this is what the architects of the *Great Reset* are aiming for. The New World Order — a name which significantly echoes the conciliar *Novus Ordo* — overturns the divine cosmos in order to spread infernal chaos, in which everything that civilization has painstakingly constructed over the course of millennia under the inspiration of grace is overturned and perverted, corrupted and canceled."[17]

Changes through the Lens of Statistics

Kenneth C. Jones wrote a book in 2003, *Index of Leading Catholic Indicators: The Church since Vatican II*, that chronicles the crisis in the Catholic Church since Vatican II. It provides a collection of statistics on vital areas of Catholic life since the 1930s. The clear conclusion is that there was a growing and vibrant Church before Vatican II — and a declining, dying Church after Vatican II. This book shows us the statistics that I know experientially to be true. The price of appeasement to the modernists and modernity as a whole was a mortal blow against the Mystical Body of Christ. As a result, the Church is in total free fall.

Perhaps the most striking statistic of all is that Sunday Mass attendance is down to about 17 percent of all Catholics in the United States right now. Before Vatican II, which ended in 1965, 75 percent of Catholics attended Mass on Sundays. (We can compare both of these numbers to the numbers in Nigeria, where a whopping 94 percent of Catholics go to Mass on Sundays — this is the country with the highest number of churchgoing Catholics.)[18] If a major company saw their regular clientele

[17]   Carlo Maria Viganò, "Viganò: Further Considerations on the Great Reset," *Catholic Family News*, May 19, 2021, https://catholicfamilynews.com/blog/2021/05/19/vigano-further-considerations-on-the-great-reset/.

[18]   Jonah McKeown, "Where Is Mass Attendance Highest? One Country Is the Clear Leader," *Catholic News Agency*, January 29, 2023, https://www.catholicnewsagency.com/news/253488/where-is-mass-attendance-highest-one-country-is-the-clear-leader.

plummet from 75 percent of the total number to only 17 percent of that number after using a new product for fifty years, everybody in leadership would be fired — including the CEO. These overall statistics paint a broad but devastating picture, and the fine details don't help to lift the spirits:

✠ Two thirds of US Catholics do not believe in the doctrine of transubstantiation, the Real Presence of Jesus Christ, Body, Blood, Soul, and Divinity in the Eucharist.

✠ Before the COVID lockdowns, one in four Catholics went to Holy Mass on Sundays. Now that the churches are open again, only about half of that 25 percent have returned to Holy Mass on Sundays. That's about one in eight Catholics who actually attend church on Sundays.

✠ For every convert to Catholicism, there are six Catholics who leave the practice of the Faith.

✠ Catholics divorce at the same rate as the rest of the culture instead of retaining the sacramental level of marriage that they are privileged to have as Catholics.

✠ In my own diocese, retired priests outnumber active priests — and there are more parishes than retired and active priests combined.

✠ Catholics publicly proclaim rights to abortion and contraception in the face of Church

teaching that identifies both practices as part
and parcel of the culture of death.

✠ Mass attendance even for those who complete
RCIA (the Rite of Christian Initiation for
Adults — i.e., the education received by adults
who are converting to Catholicism) is only
about 25 percent just three years after complet-
ing the program.

✠ The second largest "religious" group in the
United States is comprised of people who are
lapsed Catholics.

✠ Not far behind this group are the nones, who
profess no religious affiliation.

✠ There are about forty-five thousand Protestant
religious congregations that claim to believe in
Jesus Christ, but none of these churches were
actually founded by Him.

✠ Some of these Protestant congregations ap-
point women "priests or bishops." Not
surprisingly, their "vocations," like those in
the Roman Catholic Church, are in crisis
mode.[19]

In response to all of this, Raymond Arroyo has shared the results
of a nationwide survey in which Catholics in the pews voted on

---

[19] Statistics taken from *The Bellowing Ox* 10, no. 2 (March–April 2022): 3,
https://kcrd-fm.org/the-bellowing-ox.

what they think needs the most attention in the Roman Catholic Church today.[20] The top issues are as follows:

1. Better Catholic teaching and evangelization

2. Universal acknowledgement of the Real Presence of Christ in the Eucharist

3. Greater regard for the sacraments

4. Increased emphasis on marriage, the family, and the sanctity of life

5. Promotion of priestly vocations and the religious life

6. Renewed preservation of Catholic traditions — and the *Traditional Latin Mass*

Bad Liturgies

If we want to know some of the details of why people are leaving the Church in droves, we need look no further than the specific abuses that have happened within the liturgies of the NOM. These abuses steal the reverence and piety from the atmosphere of what should be a sacred place and make the sacrifice of our Lord seem like a trivial and cringeworthy sentimentality or an obscene display of blasphemies. Just as with the list of cultural degradations that we faced in the 1960s, I won't include a comprehensive accounting of these abuses here, but you can look to appendix B for a more extensive list of and references for these travesties. A few "highlights" are covered below.

---

[20] Raymond Arroyo, *The World Over*, EWTN, February 10, 2022, YouTube video, www.youtube.com/watch?v=60U5ZBbjh0U&t=1355s.

NOM priests carry on such antics as riding a scooter, wearing a wrestler's mask, using a drone to bring in the Eucharist, using an inflatable mattress as a floating altar in water, "rapping" a homily, standing and screaming like a rock star on the altar, and dancing like a DJ in front of the exposed Blessed Sacrament. In all too many places, women who are not sufficiently clothed engage in liturgical dance that is not sacred in nature. Abuses against the Blessed Sacrament are rampant; people forget that extraordinary ministers of the Eucharist are only to be used in times that are out of the ordinary, not every day. In one Italian parish, for example, someone decided it would be a good idea for very young girls, likely not even old enough to have received their First Communions, to help the priest in distributing the Eucharist. Further, demonic activity is not limited to satanic or black masses. In one instance, a witch doctor participated in a synod Mass at the cathedral in San Bernardino, California, while the bishop was present—and at a Mass in Papua New Guinea, also celebrated by a bishop, members of the congregation wore demonic masks. Just do a video search for "liturgical abuses in the Catholic Church" and prepare to weep at the display of homosexuality in the clergy and the vast panoply of profane experimentations.

For one annual event that showcases so many of these tragedies all in one place, look up the Los Angeles Religious Education Congress at the Anaheim Convention Center and watch that Mass online. It is the largest religious gathering in the world, and the modernist Catholic clergy use it as a launching pad to infiltrate every diocese in the United States. All of the liturgical innovations you experience at "St. Miscellaneous Community" or "St. Diversity's Community" started at the irreverent and modernist Los Angeles Religious Education Congress. I have personally attended several L. A. Religious Education Congresses and have witnessed the horizontal, modernist, innovative Liturgies. It's an annual weekend of hundreds of modernist speakers spreading error and heresy to the forty thousand religious education personnel for whom it is mandatory to attend, and who have heretical catechesis shoved down their throats. All the innovations at the Novus Ordo liturgy are taught and learned at the L. A. Religious Education Congress — it is ground zero. From here, attendees go back to their diocese and parishes and implement all these innovations that were taught at the L. A. Religious Education Congress. It's as if the coordinators of the L. A. Religious Education Congress want to get as far away from a traditional liturgy as possible. Why? Dr. Bill Donohue explains this succinctly in the title of an article he wrote for the website Catholic League for Religious and Civil Rights: "Traditionalism Scares Liberal Catholics." I could not agree more.

All of these liturgical abuses I've enumerated could have been prevented if only, in the years following Vatican II, we had followed the Catholic axiom *legem credendi lex statuat supplicandi* — the law of praying establishes the law of believing. In other words, the way that we pray will form what we believe. If we routinely "pray" in ways that are not sacred, ways that disrespect and blaspheme our Lord, we will no longer believe in our Lord.

Silver Linings

What can we conclude from these cultural devolutions that are mirrored in the Church, from these depressing statistics, and from these liturgical abuses? Ultimately, we are a people divided by a common religion. Some parish families are growing, some are not going to survive, and so the question remains: Will we double down on the failed ideology of modernism that has become the norm since 1965?

Further, we can ask ourselves: Are there any silver linings to the post–Vatican II Church? We know that there were modernist, communist, and Masonic dissenters and Protestant advisors who were a part of Vatican II. Be that as it may, Divine Providence was still at work at Vatican II, as it always is. By Divine Providence, I mean *God gets His way while man gets his way as well.* This is stated in the *Catechism*: "For the sake of accomplishing his plan of salvation, God permitted the acts that flowed from their blindness" (*CCC* 600). Whatever good has happened after Vatican II (despite intentional ambiguity and the modernist theologians who were invited to participate as experts) is known in medicine as *collateral circulation.* This phenomenon is something that happens naturally in the human body to protect the heart. Collateral circulation occurs when minor blood vessels enlarge to enhance circulation to compensate for damage to large vessels. Collateral circulation is the movement of blood around a blocked artery or vein by way of another path.[21] By way of analogy, the modernists at Vatican II attacked the Holy Sacrifice of the Mass, which is the heart of Catholicism. Minor blood vessels kicked in, and they have continued to bring in the grace of God to His Bride, the Church.

Some of the new blood that came out after Vatican II: EWTN; adoration chapels; the Chaplet of the Divine Mercy devotion; a resurgence in apologetics; a resurgence in Marian devotion; the pro-life movement; St. Paul Center for Biblical Theology; certain aspects of the charismatic renewal (such as fervor for reading Scripture, as well as lay involvement in healing and

---

[21] Kevin Vost, *How to Think like Aquinas* (Manchester, NH: Sophia Institute Press, 2018), 127.

deliverance teams); Theology of the Body; and orthodox Catholic publications and lay apostolates such as FOCUS, St. Joseph Communications, the Augustine Institute, LifeSiteNews, the Lepanto Institute, Catholic Answers, independent Catholic radio, and Catholic social media. The list goes on. And now there is even a resurgence of the TLM, which was almost eradicated by the modernists.

CHAPTER 3

AD ORIENTEM: HOW OUR PRIESTS LEAD THE CHURCH MILITANT IN THE BATTLE

The Priest in the Old and New Testaments

IN THE TLM, THE priest is primarily facing east, toward the risen Christ. This posture, *ad orientem*, was the position the priest took for about eighteen hundred years, in both Eastern and Western liturgies. In the way that it is preserved in the TLM, this feels like the logical extension, transformation, and fulfillment of the Old Testament sacrifices at the temple in Jerusalem. In those sacrifices, the high priest officiated *ad orientem* before the Ark of the Covenant inside the Holy of Holies and was assisted by the Levites as his acolytes. The lay people in Judaism were not allowed in the sanctuary; they were in the courtyard of the temple. In the TLM, the Catholic priest, *in persona Christi* (i.e., in the person of Christ — the Catholic priest during Mass is Christ, the everlasting High Priest), faces the tabernacle and is assisted by male acolytes or altar boys; the rest of the lay people are in the nave, just as the Jewish laity remained in the courtyard. In Sirach 50:1–21, we can read a description of this Jewish liturgy in the temple of Jerusalem, and we can see how it foreshadows the Catholic Mass:

The leader of his brethren and the pride of his people was Simon the high priest, son of Onias, who in his life repaired the house, and in his time fortified the temple. He laid the foundations for the high double walls, the high retaining walls for the temple enclosure. In his days a cistern for water was quarried out, a reservoir like the sea in circumference. He considered how to save his people from ruin, and fortified the city to withstand a siege. How glorious he was when the people gathered round him as he came out of the inner sanctuary! Like the morning star among the clouds, like the moon when it is full; like the sun shining upon the temple of the Most High, and like the rainbow gleaming in glorious clouds; like roses in the days of the first fruits, like lilies by a spring of water, like a green shoot on Lebanon on a summer day; like fire and incense in the censer, like a vessel of hammered gold adorned with all kinds of precious stones; like an olive tree putting forth its fruit, and like a cypress towering in the clouds. When he put on his glorious robe and clothed himself with superb perfection and went up to the holy altar, he made the court of the sanctuary glorious. And when he received the portions from the hands of the priests, as he stood by the hearth of the altar with a garland of brethren around him, he was like a young cedar on Lebanon; and they surrounded him like the trunks of palm trees, all the sons of Aaron in their splendor with the Lord's offering in their hands, before the whole congregation of Israel. Finishing the service at the altars, and arranging the offering to the Most High, the Almighty, he reached out his hand to the cup and poured a libation of the blood of the grape; he poured it out at the foot of the altar, a pleasing odor to the

Most High, the King of all. Then the sons of Aaron shouted, they sounded the trumpets of hammered work, they made a great noise to be heard for remembrance before the Most High. Then all the people together made haste and fell to the ground upon their faces to worship their Lord, the Almighty, God Most High. And the singers praised him with their voices in sweet and full-toned melody. And the people besought the Lord Most High in prayer before him who is merciful, till the order of worship of the Lord was ended; so they completed his service. Then Simon came down, and lifted up his hands over the whole congregation of the sons of Israel, to pronounce the blessing of the Lord with his lips, and to glory in his name; and they bowed down in worship a second time, to receive the blessing from the Most High.

The author of this passage, a contemporary of this high priest, describes in great detail and by numerous comparisons the impression of awful majesty received and the lofty joy aroused at the sight of the high priest, fully vested, entering the sanctuary, ascending the altar (vv. 6–11), and, in the presence of the whole assembly of Israel, encircled by assistant priests bearing offerings, sacrificing the burnt offering on the Day of Atonement, while the trumpets blast and the people bow down in adoration of the Most High (vv. 12–17). The hymnody, the joyful shouts of the multitude, and finally the high priest's blessing, in which he pronounces, once only in the year, on this occasion, the holy name of Yahweh, are the climax of the description of this most solemn Jewish liturgical function (vv. 18–21). As we meditate on this, let us not forget that the type and shadow, such as we see in this passage, are never greater than the reality—which is Christ in the New Covenant: the Holy Sacrifice of the Mass.

Angels and Devils

Scripture tells us that the angels worship God *ad orientem* (facing God—Matt. 18:10), while the devil and his demons turned their backs on God when they rebelled against Him. In the NOM, when the tabernacle is actually placed where it ought to be, in the center of the back wall, the priest is forced to turn his back on God and instead turn toward the people. Can you imagine how uncomfortable an orthodox priest must feel knowing that he is literally turning his back on God? In the TLM, the priest faces God, just like the angels do; in the NOM, the priest imitates the fallen angels.

In the practice of *ad orientem* liturgies, the priest is not so much facing "away from the people" as he is facing somewhere, namely, liturgical east. In facing the altar, the same direction as the congregation, his posture signifies that the whole ecclesiastical community (the Church) is offering the same sacrifice to the same and Almighty God. It is a sacrifice of syncretism and orientation toward the true God.

Anthropocentrism

When the priest faces the people, the Mass becomes a conversation between the priest and the people rather than the priest leading the people in worshipping God. Celebrated properly, the Catholic Mass is God-instituted worship; idolatry is man-instituted worship.

Putting ourselves at the center of the liturgy, also called *anthropocentrism* (i.e., being focused, or centered, on humans), is a serious problem that we have to watch out for. Unfortunately, there is far too much evidence of this in the way that most liturgies today are celebrated. Our architecture, songs and gestures, incessant announcements, and congratulatory rituals are self-referential and inwardly focused. The liturgy, as commonly celebrated, rather than as intrinsically ordered, seems more about us than about God. Even the Eucharistic Prayer, the words of which indicate that it is meant to be directed entirely to God, is usually prayed facing the people.

Pope Benedict XVI wrote on this exact subject — anthropocentrism — in his masterpiece *The Spirit of the Liturgy*:

> The turning of the priest toward the people has turned the community into a self-enclosed circle. In its outward form, it no longer opens out on what lies ahead and above, but is locked into itself. The common turning toward the east was not a "celebration toward the wall"; it did not mean that the priest "had his back to the people": the priest himself was not regarded as so important. For just as the congregation in the synagogue looked together toward Jerusalem, so in the Christian liturgy the congregation looked together "toward the Lord."[22]

He is saying that the purpose of *ad orientem* is to focus us on the One who really matters in the liturgy — the Lord — He for whom Mass is being celebrated and offered. Pope Benedict XVI continues: "On the other hand, a common turning to the East during the Eucharistic Prayer remains essential. This is not a case of something accidental, but of what is essential. Looking at the priest has no importance. What matters is looking together at the Lord."[23]

[22] Joseph Ratzinger, *The Spirit of the Liturgy* (San Francisco: Ignatius Press, 2000), 80.
[23] Ibid., 81.

Cardinal Robert Sarah has also talked about the importance of "turning toward the Lord" in liturgical worship: "Very often, our liturgies have become like theater productions. Often the priest no longer celebrates the love of Christ through his sacrifice, but just a meeting among friends, a friendly meal, a brotherly moment."[24]

The Orans Position

The orans position — the raising up of hands in the air, which is also the praying posture of the Jewish people — is almost baked into the NOM for both the priest and the people. This is despite the fact that, according to the rubrics,[25] this is a position proper only to the priest in the sacred liturgy. There is nowhere in the documents of the sacred liturgy where lay people are told to raise their hands during Holy Mass. Not surprisingly, this practice was brought into the Catholic Church in the 1960s through the charismatic renewal — which was borrowed from Protestant Pentecostals.

During the Mass, the celebrant often extends his arms in prayer, as indicated by the rubrics, but in no place are the faithful directed to do the same. This orans position of prayer has been maintained in the Catholic clergy as they lead us in the worship of God at the Holy Sacrifice of the Mass. The Church even legislates

---

[24] Christine Broesamle, trans., "Cardinal Sarah: 'How to Put God Back at the Center of the Liturgy,'" National Catholic Register, May 30, 2016, https://www.ncregister.com/news/cardinal-sarah-how-to-put-god-back-at-the-center-of-the-liturgy.

[25] *Rubrics* comes from the Latin word *ruber*, which means "red." In a missal, the prayers that the priest prays are written in black while the actions he does are written in red. The shorthand way to remember this: Say the black, do the red.

the postures of the priest and laity at Holy Mass. Pope St. John Paul II wrote the following instruction on this matter: "Neither may deacons or non-ordained members of the faithful use gestures or actions which are proper to the same priest celebrant. It is a grave abuse for any member of the non-ordained faithful to 'quasi preside' at the Mass while leaving only that minimal participation to the priest which is necessary to secure validity."[26]

This is why deacons do not raise their hands at Holy Mass—they are not *in persona Christi*. And neither are the laity. It is only the priest who is *in persona Christi*, and so only he may pray in the orans position at Mass. Outside of Mass, at a conference, at a retreat, in your private time worshipping God, you may absolutely raise your hands to God. Those are non-liturgical settings where you have freedom to express your love to God as you desire. Not only can this position be legitimate for lay people in private prayer, but it can also be very powerful!

The Point of the Spear

I find myself being drawn more and more to the traditional form of the Roman Rite. Whenever I am there, I feel like a soldier being led to battle by a general: The priest in the TLM is the tip of the spear, leading a platoon of soldiers.

The Roman army was the ancient world's master of formation movement, with a menu of predrilled movements at each Roman general's fingertips. At the cry "*Cuneum formate!*" the legionaries would form a wedge and charge at the opposition. It's a matter of

---

[26] John Paul II, "On Certain Questions Regarding the Collaboration of the Non-Ordained Faithful in the Sacred Ministry of Priest," *EWTN*, August 15, 1997, https://www.ewtn.com/catholicism/library/on-certain-questions-regarding-the-collaboration-of-the-nonordained-faithful-in-the-sacred-ministry-of-priest-2094.

simple physics. A sharp point drives deep into the body of enemy soldiers, while a thickening mass behind expands to further divide their forces. Just as a wooden wedge can split a log, a human wedge can smash an opposing force. In the Roman Empire, the tip of the wedge — the point of the spear — would be made of deep lines of the best troops, allowing for a concentration of killing power against a weaker enemy.[27] It was with this formation that Rome defeated many great armies, like that of the Greeks under Alexander the Great, and also the Britons in what is now England. It is certainly interesting to note that, with the priest at the front, the altar boys flanking him, and the congregation massing behind them, the "wedge" is the way the TLM is prayed. The architecture of this Mass facilitates this formation.

The idea of those of us who align ourselves with God belonging to His army is nothing new. We are, or ought to be, the host of Heaven. Scripture, theologians, and our popes speak within this framework again and again. In Psalm 46:8 (NABRE), for example, we read: "The LORD of hosts is with us; our stronghold is the God of Jacob." The Hebrew term *Yahweh Sabaoth* means "Lord of Hosts." It, or some close variation of it, appears 284 times in the Old Testament. This term casts God in a military light. Perhaps we don't think of Him in this way very often, but in truth, He is the leader of Heaven's armies.[28]

Dr. Scott Hahn comments on this as well: "The word 'hosts' in this context connotes military might — like 'legions' or

[27] Colin Ricketts, "3 Important Roman Military Tactics," *History Hit*, July 24, 2018, https://www.historyhit.com/roman-military-tactics/.

[28] Clarence L. Haynes Jr., "What Does It Mean That God Is 'Lord of Hosts?'," Bible Study Tools, November 16, 2021, https://www.biblestudytools.com/bible-study/topical-studies/what-does-it-mean-that-god-is-lord-of-hosts.html.

'divisions.' The Mass, it seems, is like the Normandy invasion in the spiritual realm."[29] There are few things in this day and age that strike such a martial chord as the collective memory of the D-Day invasion! Next time you are at Mass, think of that, and consider that you are in such an army, but one with a much greater purpose than freeing France of Nazi occupation. You are a soldier in an army meant to save the souls of all the world. As Pope Paul VI said, "In the earthly liturgy we take part in a foretaste of that heavenly liturgy which is celebrated in the holy city of Jerusalem toward which we journey as pilgrims, where Christ is sitting at the right hand of God.... we sing a hymn to the Lord's glory with all the warriors of the heavenly army."[30]

[29] Scott Hahn, *The Lamb's Supper* (New York: Doubleday, 1999), 140–141.
[30] Paul VI, Constitution on the Sacred Liturgy *Sacrosanctum Concilium*, no. 8, https://www.ewtn.com/catholicism/library/sacrosanctum-concilium-constitution-on-the-sacred-liturgy-1525.

CHAPTER 4

LEX ORANDI, LEX CREDENDI: THE THINGS WE DO TEACH US WHAT TO BELIEVE

The Atmosphere of the Mass

As we discussed in the first chapter, the Mass is the once and for all sacrifice of Calvary made present in the eternal now of sacred time—it is also a sacred meal (1 Cor. 5:7), in which we receive *the bread of life*, the *medicine of immortality*. Dr. Dietrich von Hildebrand wrote: "The new form of the Mass is designed to engage the celebrant and the faithful in a communal activity."[31] The NOM highlights the sacred meal aspect of the liturgy, with a detached altar in between priest and people, which comes across as looking more like a table than an altar, and all too often leads to such casual dialogue that you might be tempted to think you're sitting around the table at a Denny's restaurant. At the end of the day, the NOM is a "dialogue Mass," with occasional jokes, happy birthdays, anniversary songs, and ad-libbed prayers often added (in violation of what is licit) to spice up the service. In such a setting, you are given the Holy Eucharist, in the hand, standing up, by one of the waiters

---

[31] Dietrich von Hildebrand, "The Case for the Latin Mass," *Triumph*, October 1966, https://unavocecanada.org/wp-content/uploads/2016/01/Dietrich-Von-Hildebrand-The-Case-For-The-Latin-Mass.pdf.

on staff that day — the extraordinary ministers of Holy Communion. The average Communion at the average Catholic parish feels like a Protestant service; it does not feel mystical, mysterious, reverent, or holy. As you try to make the best of it, you find that your intellect is assaulted by the irreverence and casualness at the NOM. You continually tell yourself, "It is Jesus. It is Jesus. Just believe. Just believe." And all the while there is a battle going on in your intellect because of the lack of piety and reverence that you are witnessing. How can the Eucharist actually be Jesus when the atmosphere around Him is so casual?

But such is the case at your run-of-the-mill St. Diversity's Parish: a train of people line up in the sanctuary, behind the priest, after each one has pumped the hand sanitizer in preparation to touch and distribute the Holy Eucharist with their unconsecrated hands. Remember what happened to the layman Uzzah in the Old Testament. When he touched the Ark of the Covenant, which the Law of Moses said could be touched only by a Levite priest, God struck him dead. Scripture demonstrates that it is dangerous to act like a ministerial priest when you are not. In essence, when you act in this way, you are a fake priest. On the receiving end, you notice that the majority of people do not make an act of reverence before receiving the Eucharist, something that is actually mandated. Rather than taking a moment to bow or kneel or genuflect, most congregants will casually take the Eucharist as if it's something that's owed to them. And against all of this, you try to hold on to what you learned in your early catechism classes about the Eucharist really being Jesus' own Body, Blood, Soul, and Divinity. But everything you believe and know to be true about the Real Presence of Jesus Christ in the Holy Eucharist is attacked through your senses.

Active Participation

One of the sticking points in discussions with adherents to the NOM is that there is no room for active participation in the TLM. In the NOM, with all of the dialogue and vernacular prayers and waving and shaking of hands, people feel more physically engaged, like they are a part of what is going on. What most people don't stop to consider is that the Mass—the sacrifice on Calvary—does not need their participation to be offered. Christ's sacrifice is in no way so limited that He depends on any of us poor individuals to accomplish it. The other point that people don't realize is that you don't have to be visibly or audibly engaged to be participating in the Mass. Silent and watchful interior prayer and concentration on what the priest is doing at the altar requires a reverence and a discipline that are more focused and more to the point than any number of responses and handshakes. We don't need to follow along in books and hymnals; we can just watch in quiet adoration as Christ's sacrifice unfolds before us:

> At this point it is worth remembering that the Mass is not primarily a mental exercise. Certainly no one at Calvary was consulting a book, perhaps realizing subconsciously that the Sacrifice taking place before their eyes did not depend for its effectiveness on their own real-time intellectual comprehension of it. To be sure, it is necessary to read and reflect on Sacred Scripture, but none other than Padre Pio himself is said to have counseled that, at Holy Mass at least, the laity do not need a Missal, but would best unite themselves with the sorrows of the Blessed Virgin Mary around the foot of the Cross. That, dear reader, is what "active participation" of the laity at Mass always meant, and still means. It is

something that is best done from one's knees, and it requires less employment of the hands, the feet and the lips, and more employment of the ears and the heart, than many people realize. In spiritual terms, it is the only active participation that counts for anything.[32]

But, one might argue, the NOM "builds community." To this, Dr. Dietrich von Hildebrand responds:

Those who rhapsodize on the new liturgy make much of the point that over the years the Mass had lost its communal character and had become an occasion for individualistic worship. The new vernacular Mass, they insist, restores the sense of community by replacing private devotions with community participation. Yet they forget that there are different levels and kinds of communion with other persons. The level and nature of a community experience is determined by the theme of the communion, the name or cause in which men are gathered. The higher the good which the theme represents, and which binds men together, the more sublime and deeper is the communion. The ethos and nature of a community experience in the case of a great national emergency is obviously radically different from the community experience of a cocktail party. And of course, the most striking differences in communities will be found between the community whose theme is supernatural and the one whose theme is merely natural. The actualization of men's souls who are truly touched by Christ is the basis of a unique community, a sacred communion,

[32] "Welcome," *Usus Antiquior,* https://propria.org.

one whose quality is incomparably more sublime than that of any natural community.[33]

If you want to see an example of where real communities are being built, where the support of a natural and authentic community is fostered, nourished, and flourishing, attend a TLM parish. Unlike the majority of NOM parishes, where the pews are sparsely occupied with the elderly faithful and even more sparsely occupied by families with any great number of children, at a TLM parish you will see young, growing, faith-filled families. The back pews and vestibules are full of babies and toddlers—and their parents, who are wrangling them, one day at a time, into some understanding of and an attitude of reverence for the great mystery that they are present at. These parishes are not full of "rad trads," as faithful adherents to the TLM are sometimes and somewhat dismissively called. On the contrary, these families and communities are "glad trads."

What We Learn from Reverence and Piety

The reverence and piety in the TLM is so thick it feels as if you can cut it with a knife. Whenever I come out of the TLM, as I walk to my car in the parking lot, my soul feels like it was sandblasted with holy radiation. And sometimes I look to my wife and say, "Wow, we went to Calvary." Part of this comes from the interior silence that I experience at the TLM, which is cathartic. In that atmosphere, my soul feels protected as the priest, *in persona Christi*, prays for me for an hour, all while I am in a position of receptivity, on my knees, and in silence. Consider for a moment how often, when listening to someone speaking in a positive way about a relatively good NOM, you have heard, "It's a reverent NOM." That

---

[33]   von Hildebrand, "Case for the Latin Mass."

right there tells you there is a problem with its DNA. You can't take it for granted that you'll get a reverent NOM because the form of it doesn't guarantee it. By contrast, you never hear people say, "A reverent Latin Mass." That's because, across the board, all TLMs are reverent. It's how they're built. The movements and prayers of a TLM are precise, rich, sacred, and uniform, all leading to an overall atmosphere of reverence and piety, increasing those virtues in us when we attend in good faith.

As Dr. Dietrich von Hildebrand points out,

> In no domain is reverence more important than religion. As we have seen, it profoundly affects the relation of man to God. But beyond that it pervades the entire religion, especially the worship of God. There is an intimate link between reverence and sacredness: reverence permits us to experience the sacred, to rise above the profane; irreverence blinds us to the entire world of the sacred.... And did not the Jews tremble in deep awe when the priest brought the sacrifice into the *sanctum sanctorum, the holy of holies*? Was Isaiah not struck with godly fear when he saw Yahweh in the temple and exclaimed, "Woe is me, I am doomed! For I am a man of unclean lips … yet my eyes have seen the King?" Do not the words of St. Peter, after the miraculous catch of fish, "Depart from me, O Lord, because I am a sinner," testify that when the reality of God breaks in upon us, we are struck with fear and reverence? In a particularly striking sermon, Cardinal Newman even demonstrated that the man who does not fear and revere has not known the reality of God.[34]

---

[34] Ibid.

One of the important items that taught Catholics reverence was the altar rail. Ven. Archbishop Fulton Sheen would say that the altar rail is the ultimate form of democracy. A poor homeless Catholic can be kneeling down next to a rich Catholic, but the altar rail makes them equal. Both rich and poor have to kneel before God, humble themselves like children, open their mouths, and be fed by the priest, who feeds them like a father feeds his infant son. The sanctuary represents divinity, the nave represents humanity, and the altar rail both distinguishes between the two and gives humanity a proper way to approach divinity. The altar rail is where divinity touches humanity. It is where God communes with His children.

You might wonder if the NOM discards holy intimacy with Christ in favor of something else. And you would be right to do so:

> The [liturgical] innovators would replace holy intimacy with Christ by an unbecoming familiarity. The new liturgy actually threatens to frustrate the confrontation with Christ, for it discourages reverence in the face of mystery, precludes awe, and all but extinguishes a sense of sacredness. What really matters, surely, is not whether the faithful feel at home at Mass, but whether they are drawn out of their ordinary lives into the world of Christ—whether their attitude is the response of ultimate reverence: whether they are imbued with the reality of Christ. . . . Of course our epoch is pervaded by a spirit of irreverence.[35]

We have talked at length now about reverence, but what are we to make of piety? The Latin word for it, like the German *Pietät*, has no direct English equivalent. Briefly, we can understand it as

---

[35] Ibid.

comprising respect for tradition, honoring what has been handed down to us by former generations, and having fidelity to our ancestors and their works. Note that *pietas* is a derivative type of reverence and so should not be confused with primary reverence, which we have described as a response to the very mystery of being, and ultimately a response to God:

> A Catholic should regard his liturgy with *pietas*. He should revere, and therefore fear to abandon the prayers and postures and music that have been approved by so many saints throughout the Christian era and delivered to us as a precious heritage. To go no further: the illusion that we can replace the Gregorian chant, with its inspired hymns and rhythms, by equally fine, if not better, music betrays a ridiculous self-assurance and lack of self-knowledge. Let us not forget that throughout Christianity's history, silence and solitude, contemplation and recollection, have been considered necessary to achieve a real confrontation with God. This is not only the counsel of the Christian tradition, which should be respected out of *pietas*; it is rooted in human nature. Recollection is the necessary basis for true communion in much the same way as contemplation provides the necessary basis for true action in the vineyard of the Lord. A superficial type of communion—the jovial comradeship of a social affair—draws us out onto the periphery. A truly Christian communion draws us into the spiritual deeps.[36]

Reverence, especially when combined with a habit of recollection and contemplation, puts us on the path to true Christian

---

[36]   Ibid.

communion. While excessively inward, individualistic, and sentimental devotionalism, as has been practiced by many of us Catholics, should always be deplored, we also need to understand that the antidote to such things is not a "community experience" as such. Rather, when we are spiritually united in true reverence, in an attitude of authentic recollection, and immersed in contemplative devotion to Christ, we will discover that these things are in fact the antidote to that misplaced individualism in our spiritual communion in the Body of Christ. It is out of this attitude alone that a true communion in Christ can take place.[37]

Men Know How to Kneel

I'm a sinner. We are all sinners. When we're in church, it's best to remember this, and what we do with our bodies tells our minds what to believe. When we are at the TLM, we spend a lot of time kneeling, which is undeniably penitential. It is a biblical posture, and it's good for the soul, because, among other things, it reminds us that we're sinners in need of a Savior. When I say it's biblical, I'm thinking of the following passages, though of course there are many others:

> ✠ "The twenty-four elders fall down before him who is seated on the throne and worship him who lives for ever and ever" (Rev. 4:10).

> ✠ "[They] found Daniel making petition and supplication before his God" (Dan. 6:11).

> ✠ "And going a little farther he fell on his face and prayed, 'My Father, if it be possible, let

[37] Ibid.

this cup pass from me; nevertheless, not as I
will, but as thou wilt'" (Matt. 26:39).

✠ "At the name of Jesus every knee should bow,
in heaven and on earth and under the earth"
(Phil. 2:10).

It's not just Scripture that advises this posture. In *The Spirit of the
Liturgy*, Pope Benedict XVI writes that demons that manifested to
the Desert Fathers in the fourth century had no knees because they
are creatures full of pride. And, in "The Merit of a Mass," Fr. Ripperger writes, "The old rite fosters greater humility than the newer
rituals. This means that the newer ritual as a prayer has less of one
of the conditions that make prayer efficacious.... In this respect
the old rite is more meritorious than the new, since prayer has an
efficacy based upon how the Faith is manifested in the prayer itself."
In other words, the old rite makes you feel like you're at Calvary — as
it should, because in fact you are! Calvary is made present at your
parish, in all of our parishes, at every Mass.

In every Mass, we are attending the deathbed of Christ next
to Our Lady of Sorrows, St. Mary Magdalene, and John the
Apostle. It doesn't take much imagination to realize that such a
setting deserves weeping instead of jumping around with your
hands up in the air, hollering, "Praise the Lord!" That's just not
fitting for that eternal moment of Calvary made present. But all
too often, the new Mass makes you feel like you're at a large,
happy family meal. We need to remember that the Mass is not
entertainment; it is medicine. That's why, echoing the request of
the centurion, we say, "Lord, I am not worthy that you should
enter under my roof, but only say the word, and I shall be healed."
And, to drive home this point, Fr. Nageleisen writes: "The solemn
Mass is not instituted for the entertainment of the congregation,

or to foster the ambition of individuals, but for the purpose of moving God more effectually to grant the graces we implore; or in other words, to render the supplications and petitions of the Church more effectual."[38]

Regarding the throwing out of the old custom of kneeling not just more frequently and for longer stretches throughout the Mass but particularly when receiving Holy Communion, Dr. Dietrich von Hildebrand writes:

> Whence comes the disparagement of kneeling? Why should the Eucharist be received standing? Is not kneeling, in our culture, the classic expression of adoring reverence? The argument that at a meal we should stand rather than kneel is hardly convincing. For one thing, this is not the natural posture for eating: we sit, and in Christ's time one lay down. But more important, it is a specifically irreverent conception of the Eucharist to stress its character as a meal at the cost of its unique character as a holy mystery. Stressing the meal at the expense of the sacrament surely betrays a tendency to obscure the sacredness of the sacrifice.[39]

Look at the joint between your hip and your ankle, and remember what Pope Benedict XVI admonished, as we noted above, that one of the Desert Fathers revealed that the devils do not have knees. And then, when God blesses you, you take that blessing with deep gratitude—on your knees, spiritually and literally. You make yourself

---

[38] Fr. John A. Nageleisen, *Charity for the Suffering Souls: An Explanation of the Catholic Doctrine of Purgatory* (Charlotte, NC: TAN Books, 1994), 185.

[39] von Hildebrand, "Case for the Latin Mass."

small. In this context, consider the differences in strength, wealth, age, and sex that seem to disappear when we kneel.

The ability to kneel down before the King of Kings and Lord of Lords as we all should (Phil. 2:10–11) is a physical manifestation before God of having the faith of a child — the faith that saves you. Kneeling down is the way your soul acts through your body and practices humility. The word *humility* even comes from a Latin word, *humus*, that means "from the ground." A posture such as this was the tradition at Mass for well over a thousand years in the West.

Ultimately, when we consider this point of kneeling or not kneeling, we have to conclude that the NOM simply is not as penitential as the TLM. Rather than prolonged and calm stretches of kneeling, there is a lot more movement and activity: stand, sit, kneel, stand, sit, and so on. It's hard to give yourself over to reverent contemplation at the NOM with all the clapping, raising hands, holding hands — sometimes like a chain across the center aisle — and the sign of peace, which turns into a social hug fest. Combined with an army of extraordinary ministers of Holy Communion pumping the hand sanitizer and running around the sanctuary like little clerics, people receiving Holy Communion in their hands, or crossing their arms and receiving a blessing on their heads from a lay person — in violation of the liturgical rubrics, natural law, and biblical revelation — almost nothing about our posture at the NOM allows or fosters the reverence or penitence that ought to define our attitude at every Mass.

Sacred Music — and Its Opposite

The *sursum corda* — the lifting up of our hearts — is the first requirement for real participation in the Mass. Nothing could more effectively subvert the confrontation of man with God than the notion that we "go unto the altar of God" as we would go to a relaxing social gathering. This is why the TLM, with its Gregorian chant that raises us up to the sacred by the very nature of its specific musicality, provides a vastly superior atmosphere to that of a vernacular Mass with its popular songs, songs that leave us in a profane and merely natural atmosphere.[40] If the music at Mass makes you dance or shake your behind, it is not appropriate for Mass.

Fr. Ripperger writes, "Gregorian chant, which has an appeal to the intellect and will, naturally begets prayer, which is defined as the lifting of the mind and heart to God. Gregorian chant does not appeal to one's emotions or appetites; rather, the beauty of the chant naturally draws us into contemplation of the divine truths and the mysteries of the ritual."[41] Moreover, while the music most commonly found at the NOM is not an essential part of the newer rituals themselves, some of it is used in that context precisely because of some sensible or appetitive pleasure that can be easily derived from it — rather than for its usefulness in drawing the mind and will into closer union with God. This leads people to confuse the easy, pleasurable, and emotional experience they get from that simplistic and poorly composed music with an actual experience of God Himself. They go to Mass, the shallow music gives them an emotional experience, while obscuring their authentic encounter with Calvary, and they leave one step farther along the path that leads to thinking that God is only that shallow. Put another way, this music leads people to thinking that authentic experiences of God are always pleasant. While in the next life they

---

[40]   Ibid.

[41]   Fr. Chad Ripperger, "The Spirituality of the Ancient Liturgy," *The Latin Mass*, Fall 2001, www.latinmassmagazine.com/articles/articles_2001_FA_Ripperger.html.

are pleasant, to put it very mildly, the truth is that in this life our experiences of God are often arduous and exceedingly painful for us — not because of some defect in the way God handles us, but because of our own imperfections and sinfulness. As St. Teresa of Avila once said, "God, if this is the way you treat your friends, no wonder you have so few of them." Music — and all the other aspects of the atmosphere of this ritual that we have already discussed in this chapter — should be geared toward weaning people off sensible delights and consolations as the mainstay of their spiritual lives. God is more — and demands much more — than emotional and temporary consolations.

In case you are wondering if it's true that Gregorian chant has a sacredness to it that other music does not, listen to this. On June 5, 2021, as I walked into a convenience store, I noticed that the owners were playing Gregorian chant rather loudly from some speakers mounted outside on the roof ridge. Once I had picked up what I needed and headed to the front counter, I asked the Indian owner why they chose to play that music. His response? It was the only way to deal with a considerable problem they had faced in keeping homeless people from sleeping and panhandling in front of his store. For some reason, he said, the homeless did not like that music. It always made them leave the premises. Now, I ask you, why would homeless people have an aversion to Latin Gregorian chant? Here is my analysis: 45 percent of homeless people are mentally ill, and 50 percent of them are drug addicts.[42] Based on my experience, I believe that many of our homeless people are also diabolically afflicted. I say this because it is clear that they don't know squat about the one true Faith — Catholicism — and they

[42] "Statistics and General Information," National Coalition for the Homeless, 2023, https://nationalhomeless.org/statistics-general-information/.

are embroiled in vices that, if they understand what they are and consent to them, constitute a state of perpetual mortal sin. These two defects are a magnet for demons.

Fr. Gabriele Amorth, a noted exorcist, writes about the possession of the mentally ill:

> St. Padre Pio Pietrelcina was convinced that many persons who were admitted to psychiatric hospitals and who remained there during their entire natural life, were, in reality, possessed by the demons, and an exorcism would have been enough to cure them. This is also confirmed by the great apostle of psychiatric illnesses, the Spanish Carmelite Blessed Francis Palau. In the hospital in which he worked, he exorcised all the patients, curing many of them. This tells us something interesting: psychiatric symptoms and diabolical symptoms assume very similar forms.[43]

Remember, demons traffic in the senses, and it is because of this that Gregorian chant can dispel the demons in the air. Playing it, listening to it, hearing it, is like being on air support. With the weight of the tradition of centuries behind it, the ancient sacred music of the Catholic Church is Gregorian chant, and I have witnessed its power in action. Like spoken Latin, but only more so because sung prayer is more powerful than spoken prayer, Gregorian chant affects demons like kryptonite affects Superman.

Where do we find the opposite of Gregorian chant? Anywhere there is folksy music and liturgy. For starters, think about how Life

---

[43] Fr. Gabriele Amorth, *An Exorcist Explains the Demonic: The Antics of Satan and His Army of Fallen Angels* (Manchester, NH: Sophia Institute Press, 2016), 86.

Teen, charismatic, and other experimental Masses have flopped. Why? Maybe because you don't make worship tailored to one generation of people who are going through a temporary fad. That might have something to do with it. One of the great things about hymnody and liturgy of the past is that they reach across centuries, classes, and age groups. They have an eternal quality in their core that is not limited by or contained within any one person, time, people, or century. Remember, the Church was not invented for teenagers. The problem that we're facing here is not between old music and new music. The problem is between good music and bad music.

Rick Salbato writes:

> "When I go to Church, I don't feel anything." This has been the common cry of many of the children of the 20th century. Feelings have been what Satan has pushed in this century. Instead of spiritual reward from God, everyone wants to "feel good." The Jews looked for a physical king. Pentecostals have found a physical Holy Spirit. Sensualism is the grace of the Pentecostal movement. Everything about the Charismatics is sensual. The laying on of hands, the baptism of the spirit, the speaking in tongues, the holding of hands, the songs, the resting in the spirit and yes, even the prophecies.[44]

Feelings are not the measure of reality nor the measure of truth. The most zealous, exuberant, lively, passionate worship ever recorded in the Bible took place when the Israelites worshipped the golden calf. There was zeal, there was excitement, it was sensual, they put

---

[44] Rick Salbato, *The Tongues of Satan* (San Diego: JMJ Publications, 1983), 172.

their hands on each other, there was exuberant song — but there was no truth.

Too many people are looking at going to church as an opportunity to get entertained. Too many people want a "liver quiver." They want church to be like Burger King: "Have it your way." That's the definition of cafeteria Catholicism, and it's not a good thing. We, as Catholic Christians, need to be grounded in facts, not in feelings. But shallow contemporary Church music puts all the emphasis on mundane and profane feelings, leaving little room for elevation of the mind and heart to the factual mystery of God to which we are present. Feelings are not the measure of reality. If your faith is strictly grounded in feelings, then you are a candidate for spiritual burnout. Who ever said that Christianity was going to feel good in this lifetime? Are you supposed to feel good when you go to Holy Mass? That's not the objective. Do you think Jesus felt good when He went to the Cross? I don't think so. At Mass, we are supposed to unite ourselves with the sacrifice of Christ — the Holy Eucharist — to God the Father. Why do you think that there are the Stations of the Cross and at least one crucifix in every Catholic church? Not because we are supposed to feel slaphappy singing feel-good songs, that's for sure.

Mysterium Fidei: Does the New Mass Teach Us What We Ought to Believe?

I submit that the new liturgy must be evaluated by this test: Does it contribute to the authentic sacred community? Granted, on a human level it strives for a community character, but does it move in this direction on a higher plane? Is it a communion grounded in recollection, contemplation, and reverence? Which of the two — the NOM or the TLM, with its atmosphere of reverence, penitence, and sacred music — evokes these attitudes of soul more effectively, and thus permits a deeper and truer communion? Is it not plain that frequently the character of emphasis on the human community in the NOM is purely profane, and that, as with other social gatherings, its blend of casual relaxation and bustling activity precludes a reverent, contemplative confrontation with Christ and with the ineffable mystery of the Eucharist?[45]

If you're still not sure at the moment, that's okay. We'll revisit this question later, and hopefully by then you'll have a clear answer. As you take some time to consider what your own experiences have been at various parishes and Masses, I will share what I have learned and seen.

When have I actually experienced "the mystery of our Faith"? When have I sensed a mystical encounter with the glorified risen Christ? For me, this has happened when my soul is hearing and receiving sacred music at a High Mass, or at a Low Mass when I am enveloped in sacred silence. It has happened when I have received Holy Communion on my knees. It has happened when my hands are folded together in prayer, like the hands of Our Lady of Guadalupe in her image on the tilma. It has happened when I have knelt at an altar rail and when the paten has been placed under my chin. And it has happened when a Catholic priest, who prays for me in the language of the Church, has placed the God-Man on my tongue, like an angel placing a fiery coal into the mouth of Isaiah the prophet, purifying him. In this moment like no other, the priest at the TLM really exercises his fatherhood; he literally feeds his children the Bread of Life.

In the sacred atmosphere of the TLM, the two messiahs of Jewish expectation are revealed in the end to be one and the same:

[45] Ibid.

this priest-king, this Jesus who is at once both lamb and lion. St. Augustine said: "He endured death as a lamb and he devoured death as a lion." On our knees, we worship and tremble and trust in the presence of our great High Priest and our conquering hero. It was He who made Himself meek to such a degree that even mere mortal creatures like us may share in the spoils of His Passion, devouring in the Holy Eucharist the One who victoriously swallowed up death.

CHAPTER 5

MEN IN A MILITANT CHURCH

The Collapse of the Priesthood

SEMINARIES, THIS WORD IS derived from the Latin word *semen*, which means seminaries are to train men to inseminate the Church, the Bride of Christ with the seed of His Word. However, given the devolution of our liturgy and authentic Catholic culture over the past seventy years, should it be any wonder that the men who are on the front lines of this dumpster fire—our priests—are coming apart at the seams? Fewer and fewer young men are entering diocesan seminaries, elderly priests are not able to retire because there is no one to take their places, and it is not uncommon for priests to either walk out on the job or, as we saw in the case of Fr. Frank Pavone, be defrocked after years of confusion and battles within Church hierarchy. (Incidentally, Fr. Pavone is a defender of the TLM and has much to say about its suppression).[46] When the ship's rudder has been hampered, the officers on deck are hard-pressed to steer the vessel in the right direction. All too often, they give up hope, and after seeing their defeat and emasculation, there are not many other young men who feel emboldened to take up the fight.

---

[46] Breitbart (@wearebreitbart), "They are trying to build a world, where everyone is his or her own God," Instagram, December 30, 2023, https://www.instagram.com/reel/C1erXxird5z/?igsh=NjZiM2M3 MzIxNA%3D%3D.

Fr. John Perricone, a professor of philosophy, speaks about this implosion of the Catholic priesthood:

> This collapse was strengthened by the Nouvelle Theologie, which unleashed a model of the priesthood that was effete, saccharine and profoundly secular. The Herculean priest struggles to make men saints summoning them to spiritual warfare. He identifies false ideas and firmly condemns them. He is manfully confrontational when necessary, seeing himself as the protector of God's flock, or in the words of St. Gregory the Great, "worrying over the incursion of barbarians and fearing the wolves who menace the flock entrusted to my care." This priest after the Heart of Christ is unafraid of the heat of battle, because, through grace, his manhood remains intact; Not shredded by the jagged teeth of the Modernist Leviathan.... "The full value of this life can only be got by fighting, because if we have accepted everything, we have missed something—war. This life of ours is a very enjoyable fight, but a very miserable truce." Not so the new Post-Conciliar Priest. He preaches self-affirmation, not battle against vice. Dialogue, not refutation. Ambiguity, not truth. Massages feelings, rather than bringing men to the Cross.[47]

Women in Holy Orders

This anti-martial emasculation of priests and the role of the priesthood itself reached new depths in January of 2021, when Pope

---

[47] Fr. John Perricone, "The Priest as Hercules," *Christifideles*, November 14, 2019, https://christifideleshome.wordpress.com/2019/11/14/the-priest-as-hercules/.

Francis issued a motu proprio changing canon law to allow women to serve as lectors and acolytes.[48] In *Spiritus Domini*, he changed canon 230, §1 of the Code of Canon Law to read: "Lay people who have the age and skills determined by decree of the Episcopal Conference, can be permanently assumed, through the established liturgical rite, to the ministries of lectors and of acolytes; however this contribution does not give them the right to support or to remuneration by the Church."

Prior to this change, the law said, "Lay men who possess the age and qualifications established by decree of the conference of bishops can be admitted on a stable basis through the prescribed liturgical rite to the ministries of lector and acolyte."

The roles of lector and acolyte are publicly recognized ministries instituted by the Church and traditionally were understood to be "minor orders." That is, in the tradition of the Church, they were a spiritual and functional precursor to the priesthood itself. As priests are our fathers, and women can neither biologically, psychologically, or spiritually be fathers—just as men can in no way, shape, or form be mothers—these minor orders have previously only been held by men. It was even written into Church law: "Before anyone is promoted to the permanent or transitional diaconate, he is required to have received the ministries of lector and acolyte."

What are men to do when the pope himself undercuts their role as men, when his actions falsely imply that men are not needed because women can do what, according to the natural order of distinct and God-given gifts to men on the one side and women on the other, only men can do? To say that such circumstances are

---

[48] Courtney Mares, "Pope Francis Admits Women to Ministries of Lector and Acolyte in New Motu Proprio," *Catholic News Agency*, January 11, 2021, https://www.catholicnewsagency.com/news/246027/pope-francis-admits-women-to-ministries-of-lector-and-acolyte-in-new-motu-proprio.

disheartening is putting it mildly. To say that such "leadership" is scandalous and intrinsically damaging is more accurate.

An Existential Clash: Men and Effeminate Priests

When men are told that there is little or no room for authentic masculinity in the priesthood, only effeminate men will be interested in becoming priests. What is the result? It is a cascading effect, caused by poor leadership, from the top down, of the men who ought to be in congregations leaving in droves because they see no masculine leadership in the pulpit. *Lex orandi, lex credendi.* What they see every day is what forms their belief. If they see an emasculated Church, they will think that there is no room for authentic masculinity in the Church. And so, following the natural and good instinct that every man has to be a real man, they will walk away.

In a clarion call that speaks in the face of this disaster, Fr. John Perricone again gives us an image of what a real priest is, what he can be, what he ought to be:

> As Hercules, the priest is given strength from Heaven beyond ordinary human capacities. Hercules willingly embraced his twelve labors, bravely overcoming their wickedness. Similarly, the priest encounters the gates of Hell. Clothed in Christ's sacerdotal armature the priest — as alter Christus — vanquishes Hell's terrors with the invincible power of the sacraments. Hercules is always depicted by rippling mounds of muscle. The priest enjoys a more formidable notice, his heroic virtue, which amazes the world more than Hercules' imposing physical frame.

This dogmatic picture of the priest has been obscured by the Great Crisis of the past two decades. In fact, the attenuation of the priest reaches back for some 50 years. After the Second Vatican Council many thought the priest's sacred character ill fitted to modernity's Brave New World. The theological class bullied bishops into accepting a new paradigm of the priest as political actor, social activist, and throughout the South American church, guerrilla Marxist.[49]

Role Models for Parish Priests

To whom should these men in the congregation look if they cannot find priests who are authentically masculine in their own parishes? To whom should faithful seminarians and priests look as they seek proper formation for themselves? Again, we turn to the wise words of Fr. John Perricone, who reminds us of the patron saint of parish priests:

> No one was more Hercules than the Cure of Ars, St. John Mary Vianney. This 19th century saint never left his parish of Ars, France. All he did was offer Mass, hear Confessions and teach the Catechism. Of course, that's like saying all that MacArthur and Patton did was defeat the Axis powers. St. John Vianney engaged men at the only place that matters — the battlefield of their souls. He helped them conquer their sins, and so helped them be men again. No joy compares to that joy.
>
> In another time, that is the only kind of priest the world knew. So much so that a 1954 Hollywood produced *On*

---

[49] Perricone, "The Priest as Hercules."

the Waterfront. The world was richer when such priests strode the earth. How much poorer it is without them. How much more dangerous.[50]

These priests that Fr. Perricone speaks of were the priests who were formed and served in the context of the TLM, which, by its very nature, inspired them to discipline, paternity, order, and beauty. In the enervation of the Mass that we have seen since the travesty of Vatican II, our priests — and so too our men — have lost their purpose. They no longer know which way to look or how to act, and they either have been cut off or have willingly cut themselves off to look for fulfillment and purpose in lesser and fruitless ways, none of which will ultimately model for them or restore to them the masculinity that they seek.

Contemplative Prayer: Men Are Made to Run, Not Walk

In 1 Corinthians 9:24, St. Paul admonishes us, "Do you not know that in a race all the runners compete, but only one receives the prize? So run that you may obtain it." How, as men, can we run the spiritual race in such a way as to win the prize of eternal union with God?

No man — priest or layman — can be the man he was made to be unless he forms his desires, focus, and purpose by regular prayer. Ven. Archbishop Fulton Sheen, in speaking of the three forms of prayer, says that vocal prayer is like going to God on foot, meditative prayer is like going to God on horseback, and contemplative prayer is like going to God on a jet.[51] At the TLM, we can

---

[50] Ibid.
[51] Fulton Sheen, *Your Life Is Worth Living* (New York: Image, 2019), 398.

enter immediately into meditative and contemplative prayer and stay there throughout the Mass. This is almost impossible in the NOM, where sacred silence is so hard-pressed to find a home.

Catholic tradition even tells us that the highest form of prayer is in fact contemplative prayer — well, the TLM is almost entirely contemplative prayer for lay Catholics, especially if they are not using missals. When I am there, I know that the priest is praying to God on his own and on my behalf, and I just close my eyes, and I can see a tidal wave of actual and sanctifying grace washing over me. It's like standing underneath a holy waterfall. The sacred silence in the TLM allows me to contemplate God, Heaven, the angels, my beloved dead, the afterlife, my particular judgment, the joy of salvation, the meaning and purpose of life, and everything else that matters to such a degree as all of these.

Contemplative Prayer in Scripture

One of the key sources of formation, always and everywhere, for every man, is Sacred Scripture. As we are discussing the value of contemplative prayer and its ability to bring us right to God, it is essential to consider what Scripture says about being silent in the presence of the Lord. This is by no means an exhaustive list of verses on the subject, but if you are getting to the point where contemplative prayer seems more difficult and less fruitful than you would wish, you can return to these verses for reassurance and encouragement to keep on keeping on with it.

> ☩ "Be still before the Lord, and wait patiently for him; fret not yourself over him who prospers in his way, over the man who carries out evil devices" (Ps. 37:7).

✠ "But the LORD is in his holy temple; let all the earth keep silence before him" (Hab. 2:20).

✠ "Be silent, all flesh, before the LORD; for he has roused himself from his holy dwelling" (Zech. 2:13).

✠ "Be silent before the Lord GOD! For the day of the LORD is at hand; the LORD has prepared a sacrifice and consecrated his guests" (Zeph. 1:7).

✠ "And there he came to a cave, and lodged there; and behold, the word of the LORD came to him, and he said to him, 'What are you doing here, Eli'jah?' He said, 'I have been very jealous for the LORD, the God of hosts; for the people of Israel have forsaken thy covenant, thrown down thy altars, and slain thy prophets with the sword; and I, even I only, am left; and they seek my life, to take it away.' And he said, 'Go forth, and stand upon the mount before the LORD.' And behold, the LORD passed by, and a great and strong wind rent the mountains, and broke in pieces the rocks before the LORD, but the LORD was not in the wind; and after the wind an earthquake, but the LORD was not in the earthquake; and after the earthquake a fire, but the LORD was not in the fire; and after the fire a still small voice. And when Eli'jah heard it, he wrapped his face in his mantle and went out and stood at the entrance of the cave. And behold, there came a voice to him, and said, 'What are you doing here, Elijah?'" (1 Kings 19:9–13).

Contemplative Prayer in the Writings of the Saints and Our Contemporaries

Just as Scripture is an invaluable source of wisdom, direction, and encouragement for us, so too are the examples, lives, and writings of the saints. Clearly, their prayer lives led them to Heaven and union with God. We would be smart to listen to what they have to say on the subject! As with the Scripture verses above, you can turn back to this collection of quotations anytime your contemplative prayer life needs a kick in the pants.

✠ "What we need most in order to make progress is to be silent before this great God with our appetites and our tongue, for the language He best hears is silent love" (St. John of the Cross).

✠ "The sixth mansion is known as the 'prayer of quiet,' which is a type of mystical, infused contemplation" (St. Teresa of Avila).

✠ "In the silence of the heart God speaks. If you face God in prayer and silence, God will speak to you.... It is only when you realize your nothingness, your emptiness, that God can fill you with Himself. Souls of prayer are souls of great silence" (St. Teresa of Calcutta).

✠ "O my Jesus, you alone know the longings and sufferings of my heart. I am glad I can suffer for you, however little. When I feel that the suffering is more than I can bear, I take refuge in the Lord in the Blessed Sacrament, and I speak to him with profound silence" (St. Faustina Kowalska).

Picking up where these saints left off, and speaking specifically about room for silence in the Mass itself, Fr. Ripperger says:

> The new rite, as a form of prayer, is hard to pray mentally since there are more things said out loud, and the general tenor of Vatican documents on the subject encourages a form of active participation that requires more things occurring on the side of the laity. The old Mass, since it is less activist on the side of the laity, tends to make it easier for them to pray the Mass. While the old rite stresses a more interior active participation, the new rite, with a lack of periods of silence as exist in the old rite, makes the ritual less meditative. In fact, the periods of meditation in the new rite are somewhat artificial and are not integral to the ritual as such but serve to stop the ritual rather than being a part of it. . . . As a result, in the new rite it is harder for people to lift their minds and hearts to God. The requirement of attention as part of prayer is more difficult and so, in that respect, the new rite is less meritorious than the old because God is more pleased with those things that easily draw us to Him.[52]

The best way I can describe the TLM is to say that actions speak louder than words. The actions at a silent low TLM speak loudly

---

[52] Fr. Chad Ripperger, "The Merit of a Mass," *The Latin Mass*, Spring 2003, https://unavocecanada.org/wp-content/uploads/2017/05/The-Merit-Of-A-Mass.pdf.

to the human soul. In this context, we can know without a doubt that "right worship itself is a cause of grace."[53]

Vocal Prayer in the NOM

The NOM takes me to God on foot because it is more of a dialogue Mass, meaning there is not enough time for silent and contemplative prayer. Father prays, we pray. Father says one thing, we say something else. The only time I find that I can start going into contemplative prayer at the NOM is after I receive Holy Communion, when I go and kneel down and begin to contemplate this mystical union between my soul and the Eucharistic Lord. However, this window of time is usually very short because, invariably, the choir will start playing that folksy '70s and '80s chromatic liturgical music with winged instruments that ignite the passions and disrupt the sacred silence.

While we have discussed this point before, it bears repeating not just because it matters that music be sacred or not sacred, but also because this music that is not sacred does not just fail to serve as a vehicle to carry our minds and hearts to God. Far worse, it is such profane noise and distraction that, far from being neutral rather than positive, it is actually a negative. It makes it harder for us to pray at all, let alone to enter into contemplative prayer. The cacophony of effeminate songs are oftentimes heretical, or the music is horizontal (we sing about the community) instead of being vertical (that is, singing about and worshipping God). The songs at the NOM are very often written by poorly formed modernists, some of whom are openly

---

53 Whispers of Restoration, "Worship with Non-Catholics: Can You Do It?," *OnePeterFive*, February 27, 2018, https://onepeterfive.com/worship-non-catholics/.

sexual degenerates. And, as though this were not enough to inhibit prayer, very often the choir is taken from the back of the church, where they used to be hidden in the choir loft, and placed up front, on the side of the sanctuary. Instead of their singing being an anonymous and sacred gift and prayer, it feels like a performance, with the people in the nave clapping along, raising their hands, snapping their fingers, bobbing their heads to the beat, and tapping their toes. When a song is finished, especially at the end of Mass, many congregations will applaud the choir as though a concert really did just finish up. A sobering thought for you to chew on next time you're at a Mass with such antics going on: St. Padre Pio was once asked what the problem was with clapping at Mass. He answered, "In Calvary, there were those applauding Christ's death: the Sanhedrin, soldiers and demons." While you let that sink in, remember that the music at Mass must be a prayer, not a performance. It must enhance our ability to enter into contemplative prayer, not take away from it. And at the TLM, the choir is in the loft, or at least in the back of the church if there is no loft, and the music is sacred and chanted (sometimes accompanied by an organ). Where possible, a men's schola provides the chant, and it is strong, martial, serious, and masculine.

With a paternal commanding officer to lead the charge as the tip of the spear, surrounded by the discipline of reverence and piety, demonstrating fealty and humility to our Lord and King in kneeling before Him while he strives to run to Him in contemplative prayer, and lifted up closer to Him by the timeless and rock-solid depth of Gregorian chant, every layman can know at the TLM that this is a place where he can, authentically and without apology, give himself over to the masculine nature that God gave to him at the moment he came into existence. And by that simultaneous surrender and answer to carry the banner in the battle, each man at the TLM, each time he is there and willing, comes one step closer to eternal union with God.

CONCLUSION TO PART I

WE'VE COVERED A LOT of ground over the past five chapters. We've talked about what the Mass is, what happened to it and to our society in the 1960s to land us where we are today, how our postures and the overall atmosphere of the Mass inform how and what we believe, and why the TLM is suited for men in a way that the NOM is not.

So now it's time to ask yourself again that question we asked a little earlier: Is the new Mass teaching us what we ought to believe? And if you're still not sure, let's remember some of those things that have happened at new Masses that we talked about earlier on and that you can read more about in the resources in appendix B. While it might be temporarily comforting to dismiss these abuses with a plea that they only happened because people misinterpreted or misapplied the "well-intentioned" "reforms" of Vatican II, remember that our shepherds in the Church have a duty to maintain such a level of clarity in their guidance that grievous errors such as these should never have had the leeway to happen. Discard that comforting excuse of good intentions, remember the old saying about where such good intentions lead, and be emboldened by the call to cast aside anything so unworthy of a man of God. You were not made for comfort—you were made for greatness. As you read through those atrocities, ask yourself: Are these things that inspire me to greater reverence, piety, respect, and soldierly affection for my King and Lord? Or do they seem weak and foolish? Do they nourish a sense of courage and respect, or do they hide the sacrifice of Christ on the Cross behind an embarrassing show of human-centric and profane performance? Do they prompt me to love God more, or do they make me want to throw up my hands and walk away from the Mass?

Dr. Dietrich von Hildebrand asked the question best: "Does the new Mass, more than the old, bestir the human spirit—does it evoke a sense of eternity? Does it help raise our hearts from the concerns of everyday life—from the purely natural aspects of the world—to Christ? Does it increase reverence, an appreciation of the sacred? Of course, these questions are rhetorical, and self-answering."[54]

If you feel conflicted, as though you are convinced of the superiority of the TLM but are not ready to "let go" of the NOM, which is likely more familiar to you, don't worry about it. In this unfortunate situation that we find our Church in today, you have your hard-line TLM-only Catholics, and you have your entrenched NOM Catholics, who insist that we must follow the mainstream Church. However, I consider myself part of a third camp. This is the demographic of Catholics who say, "I accept both forms of the Mass." I agree with Dr. Scott Hahn, who says: "We've [Catholics] got to recognize the validity of the Novus Ordo Mass.... We can also recognize the objective superiority of the Traditional Latin Mass."[55] The fact that the TLM is superior does

[54] Dietrich von Hildebrand, "The Case for the Latin Mass," *Triumph*, October 1966, https://unavocecanada.org/wp-content/uploads/2016/01/Dietrich-Von-Hildebrand-The-Case-For-The-Latin-Mass.pdf.

[55] Scott Hahn, "Scott Hahn on the Latin Mass" in *Pints With Aquinas* with Matt Fradd. https://www.youtube.com/watch?v=WKVMIpH77Hc/. Accessed 06/25/2024.

not mean that the NOM is not still the actual sacrifice of Jesus on Calvary. It is still that, despite all the offenses against Him that happen in its profane atmosphere and misleading rubrics.

What we have today in the NOM is the same confusion that the Israelites had in the days of the Judges (21:25): "In those days there was no king in Israel; every man did what was right in his own eyes." Today, we have *the modernist spirit of Vatican II* where every diocese, every parish, every liturgy committee, celebrates the Mass according to *what is right in their own eyes.* As I noted in the preface, St. Paul tells us in 1 Corinthians 14:33, "God is not a God of confusion but of peace." Yet in our Church as it is now, we do not have this peace. There is no uniformity; there is liturgical confusion and conflict. Which makes me think about a joke I once heard, one that seems to be absolutely true: "What's the difference between a liturgist and a terrorist? You can negotiate with a terrorist." This strident inability to communicate within our own Church about the very Sacrifice of the Mass that is the heart of our Church tells me that the DNA of the NOM is defective. It has not been repaired, or maybe it can't be repaired. One thing I do know is that repairing it is above my pay grade.

Pope Benedict XVI, Fr. Joseph Fessio, the EWTN TV Mass, and a few other notable individuals and outlets have tried to promote the "reform of the reform," which would mean implementing the NOM precisely as the Council wrote down. The best description I have seen of what this would look like comes from Fr. Fessio in his article "The Mass of Vatican II," which he published with *Catholic World Report* on December 7, 2023, and which you can read in its entirety on their website.[56] (Much of that article is

---

[56] Fr. Joseph Fessio, "The Mass of Vatican II," *Catholic World Report*, December 7, 2023, https://www.catholicworldreport.com/2023/12/07/the-mass-of-vatican-ii/.

included in chapter 7 of this book.) Quite possibly the last hope we had as a universal Church to get the Vatican II Mass corrected liturgically was under the papacy of Benedict XVI. But now that he is gone, that possibility is likely gone as well. And so we will continue to see virtually every parish Mass have its own nuances and slight differences as each parish implements the NOM as it sees fit — and all too often that means abuses and irreverent degradations in personal liturgical agendas.

TLM parishes are small in number, but they are still much more available now than they were for decades, thanks to Pope Benedict XVI's motu proprio *Summorum Pontificum*, which he released in July 2007. This specified the circumstances in which priests of the Roman Rite may celebrate Mass according to the "Missal promulgated by Blessed John XXIII in 1962" (which was the latest edition of the Roman Missal in the form most commonly known as the Tridentine Mass, Extraordinary Form, or TLM). Essentially, this opened the doors for much wider celebration of the TLM, and in the years immediately following this direction, communities that had tried to preserve it through the darkest years of the '70s, '80s, and '90s felt again that they were part of the Church. Pope Benedict XVI removed the TLM from a marginalized status and quite literally gave it an extraordinary status when he coined the term *Extraordinary Form* of the Roman Rite.

Today, the primary religious orders of priests who offer the TLM are the Priestly Fraternity of St. Peter and the Institute of Christ the King Sovereign Priest. These traditionalist orders are in communion with Rome, and they accept the legitimacy of Vatican II and the NOM, while obviously living their lives by the TLM. There are also diocesan priests in most dioceses who offer the Latin Mass, and their number is growing. You just have to shop around. However, Pope Francis has supplanted *Summorum Pontificum* with his new motu proprio on the traditional Latin Mass called *Traditionis Custodes* released in 2021. There is a new Vatican document that is being prepared by Cardinal Víctor Fernández, head of the Dicastery for the Doctrine of the Faith, which would impose still tighter restrictions on the celebration of the Traditional Latin Mass.

Now that you know what you are looking for, and why you are looking for it, all you have left to do is commit yourself to finding it and sticking by it. In all endeavors, great and small, we ask the saints to help us do what we ought, to be bold in our pursuit of Christ as they were. St. Pius V, restorer of the beauty of the sacred liturgy, *ora pro nobis*. St. Pius X, foe of modernism, *ora pro nobis*. St. Anthony, hammer of heretics, *ora pro nobis*. St. Francis of Assisi, rebuilder of the Church, *ora pro nobis*. *Ave Maria, ora pro nobis*.

PART II

Introduction: From the Experts

In the previous chapters, I shared with you many relatively short quotations from Scripture, the saints, and various more contemporary theologians and writers to help illustrate the points I was making. But there are three articles that are so helpful in understanding all of this that this second part of the book is dedicated to sharing them—almost in their entirety—with you. Naturally, I am very grateful to these authors for two things: first, for the wisdom that they shared in the original publication of these words, and second, for their generosity in allowing me to include them in this book.

In an effort to make this material more approachable, I've broken it down into a question-and-answer format. All of the questions are from me; all of the answers are the authors' own and original words. I will begin with an article from Fr. Chad Ripperger, an exorcist and priest whom I quoted a lot in part I. Next, we'll look at an article from Fr. Joseph Fessio, another priest I referenced a few times in part I. Finally, we'll look to lawyer Christopher Ferrara. Given his profession, he has the technical expertise to tease out these matters in a somewhat unique way.

I hope that you will find the insights of these three men as helpful as I have. Please note that any boldface is an emphasis that I have added to highlight certain facts and ideas for you, while anything in brackets is my commentary, not from the original authors.

CHAPTER 6

"The Merit of a Mass" by Fr. Chad Ripperger, F.S.S.P.[57]

What type of value do we derive from Holy Mass, and how much value does Holy Mass give us?

We must … sharply distinguish between the intrinsic and the extrinsic value of the Mass. As for its intrinsic value, it seems beyond doubt that, in view of the infinite worth of Christ as the Victim and High Priest in one Person, the sacrifice must be regarded as of infinite value, just as the sacrifice of the Last Supper and that of the Cross.

Is the "extrinsic value" of the Mass limited?

While we must always regard its intrinsic value as infinite, since it is the sacrifice of the God-Man Himself, its extrinsic value must necessarily be finite in consequence of the limitations of man. The scope of the so-called "fruits of the Mass" is limited.

What is the distinction between the intrinsic value and the extrinsic value of the Mass?

In discussing the value of the Mass, one must make a distinction between the intrinsic and the extrinsic value. The intrinsic value

---

[57] Fr. Chad Ripperger, "The Merit of a Mass" *The Latin Mass*, Spring 2003, 21–31.

of any valid Mass is infinite since it is Christ, Who is infinite, Who is offered. Hence, in this respect every Mass has an infinite value. The new rite of Mass is just as efficacious as the old rite of Mass in this respect since they are both the same sacrifice of Christ. The Mass, because it is the offering of God the Son to God the Father, gives infinite glory to God. However, the extrinsic value or merit of the Mass is finite.

Does man receive infinite effects from the fruits of the Mass?

Man, a finite creature, is incapable of receiving infinite effects. In this respect, the value of the Mass is "intensive limited," which means that the fruit of the Mass is limited in its measure. Normally, the liturgical writers state that, as to its impetratory and expiatory value, the Mass is finite, "since the operations of propitiation and impetration refer to human beings, who as creatures can receive a finite act only."

I thought the effects of the Mass were infinite?

When one considers the actual sacrifice of the Mass, which is the sacrifice of Calvary, it is infinite, but as to its effects, other than the infinite effect of giving God glory, it is finite. In addition to man's finitude, the liturgical writers give other reasons for the limitation of the extrinsic value of the Mass. **While the Mass is infinite as to What is sacrificed, nevertheless we derive only finite fruits from the Mass**. "They (the laity at Mass) will receive grace in the measure of their faith and devotions visible to God alone" (Roman Missal, Angelus Press 1962, p. 885).

How does the Church affect the extrinsic merits of the Mass?

If the actual members of the Church are not very holy their lack of holiness has a direct impact on the efficacy of the Mass, since the Mass is offered always as a public prayer, even when it is offered privately. Given the current scandals in the Church among the clergy and bishops, we can begin to see why the faithful are suffering spiritually. The same can be said for mankind as a whole, since the fruits of the Mass can also be applied for those who are not Catholics. The moral and spiritual depravity of this moment in history has gravely affected this aspect of merit in the Church.

How does the priest as private person affect the extrinsic merits of the Mass?

If, therefore, the celebrant be a man of great personal devotion, holiness, and purity, there will accrue an additional fruit which will benefit not himself alone, but also those in whose favor he applies the Mass. The faithful are thus guided by sound instinct when they prefer to have Mass celebrated for their intentions by an upright and holy priest rather than by an unworthy one, since, in addition to the chief fruit of the Mass, they secure this special fruit which springs *ex opere operantis*, from the piety of the celebrant.... This is why the holiness of the clergy has a direct impact on the life of the Church. **If the priests are holy, the fruits derived from the Masses they offer are greater and the Church's faithful benefit more thereby. This is also why the faithful have a certain sense that it is better to have a holy priest rather than an unholy priest offer the Mass for their intentions.** The fact is that the Mass said by a good priest is better and more efficacious than the Mass said by a bad priest. How the priest offers the Mass also increases merit insofar as it is more meritorious if he offers the Mass reverently rather than irreverently.

[Fr. Ripperger's words on this point call to mind this Old Testament passage about offering God polluted food on the sacrificial altar: "And you say, 'How have we polluted it?' By thinking that the LORD's table may be despised. When you offer blind animals in sacrifice, is that no evil? And when you offer those that are lame or sick, is that no evil? Present that to your governor; will he be pleased with you or show you favor? says the LORD of hosts" (Mal. 1:7–8). The Levite priests were sacrificing animals forbidden by the Law of Moses. Leviticus 22:22 explicitly says that blind animals are not to be offered. Neither are lame or diseased animals. Yet these are the kinds of offerings being brought to the Lord. The point is that the Levite priests know that they are offering God their leftovers instead of their best animals, and this displeases God. This passage of Malachi is addressed to Israel's spiritual leaders, who are being lazy and disrespectful and are not following the prescribed rules of the Old Testament liturgy.]

How do the faithful affect the extrinsic merits of the Mass?

This also means that if the faithful have a higher degree of virtue and grace, they will be able to merit more from the Mass.... The more fervent the prayer, the richer the fruit.... On a pastoral level, this means that the holier the congregation, the more they will be able to merit and therefore the better will be the pastoral life of both priest and faithful. Conversely, **if any of the faithful are in the state of mortal sin, it affects everyone else.**... In an even worse scenario, if they are receiving Holy Communion in the state of mortal sin, they detract from the goodness of the Mass extrinsically and in this way affect everyone else. This is why the problem of the state of the faithful is such an important issue. The fact that a vast majority of Catholic couples are using contraception as well as the general moral and spiritual decay among the faithful in virtually all areas has left this aspect of merit regarding the Mass anemic, to say the least. Dr Ludwig Ott observes (*Fundamentals of Catholic Dogma*, p. 415) that **the merit derived from the Mass on the part of the faithful does not work mechanically but is based upon the dispositions of the faithful. Also, the liturgical writers also indicate that the fruits of the Mass can be received more efficaciously by those properly disposed than by those not properly disposed.**

[If lay people are not properly catechized (a word that means "Christian instruction"), they are at risk of finding the Mass unintelligible at best and boring at worst. The Church specifies that "'the Sacred Liturgy does not exhaust the entire activity of the Church.' It must be preceded by evangelization, faith, and conversion. It can then produce its fruits in the lives of the faithful" (*CCC* 1072). In order for adults to experience the intended fruits of the Mass, they must be evangelized; they must have had that intimate sacred encounter with our Lord.]

How does beauty affect the extrinsic merits of the Mass?

If we use objects that do not fit the majesty and the exalted nature of the Holy Sacrifice of the Mass, we can actually detract from the extrinsic merit. Ugly things please God less and thus merit less. Also, if we give with the intention of being cheap, we tell God what we really think of Him — that retention of our money is more important than His glory.... Often those who offer the new rite use ugly items because they think to do so pleases God. They argue based on the notion of simplicity (which we have already shown in a prior article is not a valid argument). Simplicity is not the same thing as ugliness. The truly magnificent church or liturgical object pleases God both in itself and because a magnificent item more easily moves people to lift their minds and hearts to Him. Objectively, then, we can say that offering Mass in a magnificent church with the vestments and sacred vessels that suit the level of Mass offered will derive the most extrinsic merit regarding the decora.... On the other hand, lack of beauty in the decora will reduce the extrinsic merit. Also, not saying Mass in a church will reduce the merit of the Mass. This does not mean that a priest should forego offering Mass if he cannot get to a church, since there are all kinds of circumstances which may warrant not saying Mass in a church. **Nevertheless, a Mass offered in a beautiful church is more meritorious. On a practical level, the laity and clergy must insist that the church and other decora be beautiful and properly suited to the Mass. This is not just a matter of aesthetics.... It is a matter of spiritual import since it can directly affect the merit of the Mass.... There is probably no layman who has not noticed the differences in their experiences of the Mass when they attended an ugly church as opposed to a beautiful one.**

How does the merit of the ritual itself affect the extrinsic merits of the Mass?

Another reason one ritual can be more efficacious than another is that it is offered with greater solemnity or, as Nicholas Gihr (liturgical expert) puts it, pomp. The solemnity and pomp give greater glory to God, and are eminently suited to Him since He is the Majesty or Ruler of the whole universe. He is greater than any earthly king and therefore deserves a greater ritual than any earthly king. St. Thomas names: humility and faith. Humility is necessary because we must recognize our unworthiness. Faith is necessary in order for us to know Who and What God is, so that we act rightly. Here the principle of *lex credendi lex orandi* ["the law of what is prayed is the law of what is believed"] plays a key role. St. Thomas says that prayers must be offered to God and with devotion. Lastly, for the prayer to be meritorious, the person must be in the state of grace.... **The new rite is "streamlined" in the sense that those who wrote it sought to simplify the ritual. This resulted in less pomp, so in this respect we may say the old rite is more meritorious than the new.... The old rite is more ordered to God and less ordered toward the people. This is manifest not only in altar orientation (the new rite can be said oriented) but also in the fact that references to the supernatural were reduced in the propers....** The ritual of the Mass ought to be ordered to God and not to man, except insofar as man is served in order to serve God. In other words, God is the end of the ritual, not man.

Are the prayers in the old rite more beautiful than the prayers in the new Mass?

In connection to the clarity of faith, we have also seen that the old rite is more beautiful than the new. The more beautiful a thing is, the more it pleases God.... The prayers of the old rite of Mass better express the desires and intentions of an authentic Catholic faith, since they contain the faith in a clearer fashion. The prayers of the old rite of Mass foster a greater sense of our unworthiness and need for humility and sorrow for our sins. The prayers are more ordered toward God and suit Him better since they contain a proper supernatural dimension.

[Dr. Peter Kwasniewski says: "The content of the two missals is different.... The content is the deeper problem. The prayers have been edited to reflect a 1960s point of view—the prayers themselves. Only 13 percent of the prayers or the orations from the old Missal (pre-1962) made it into the new Missal intact. That's not continuity.... These prayers are the Collect, the Secret, and the Postcommunion, what they now call the Collect, the Prayer over the Offerings, and the Prayer after Communion."[58]]

[58] Dr. Peter Kwasniewski, "Given a Choice, Why Should I Consistently Attend the Traditional Latin Mass?," November 6, 2021, St. Thomas Aquinas Catholic Church, Charlotte, NC, YouTube video, https://www.youtube.com/watch?v=m2fM4ZkzzPs.

CHAPTER 7

"THE MASS OF VATICAN II" BY FR. JOSEPH FESSIO, S.J.[59]

Fr. Joseph Fessio, arguably the best apologist and the most outspoken priest pushing for "the reform of the reform" of the Vatican II Mass, is the founder of Ignatius Press. He entered the Jesuit novitiate in 1961 and was ordained a priest in 1972. He received a doctorate in theology in 1975 from the University of Regensburg, West Germany, where his thesis director was then-Fr. Joseph Ratzinger. His celebration of the NOM is very reverent; it looks like the TLM in English with many of the prayers, chants, doxologies, and antiphons still in Latin, and it incorporates authentic sacred music. The modernists have an aversion to it because they say it resembles the TLM, and the trads have an aversion to it because it was the fruit of Archbishop Annibale Bugnini, the modernist Freemason instrumental in Vatican II. This is an abridged version of Fr. Fessio's original article.

What is the Vatican II document on the New Order of the Mass?

The Constitution on the Sacred Liturgy, *Sacrosanctum Concilium*, was one of two documents issued on the same day, December

---

[59]   Fr. Joseph Fessio, "The Mass of Vatican II," *Catholic World Report*, December 7, 2023, https://www.catholicworldreport.com/2023/12/07/the-mass-of-vatican-ii/.

4, 1963, the first two documents issued by the Second Vatican Council.

Has Sacrosanctum Concilium been successfully implemented?

Sacrosanctum Concilium is one of the most important documents of the Council, one that has been the least understood and, I believe, has wrought the most havoc — not by having been fulfilled — but by having been ignored or misinterpreted.

What was the central intent of Vatican II concerning the sacred liturgy?

Now there should be no argument about the central intent of the Council concerning the liturgy. The Council actually spells out its intent, in paragraph 14 of *Sacrosanctum Concilium*: "Mother Church earnestly desires that all the faithful should be led to that full, conscious, and active participation in liturgical celebrations, which is demanded by the very nature of the liturgy." **The key words here are "full, conscious, and active participation." The Latin for "active participation" is *actuosa participatio*.**

What does the term active participation mean in light of prior Church usage?

I did a little research into previous uses of that expression in papal and other ecclesial documents. The first papal usage was in 1903 by Pope St. Pius X, whose motto was "*Omnia Instaurare in Christo*" (To restore all things in Christ). He considered himself a pope of renewal. He was elected in August of 1903 and in November, he issued one of the first documents of his pontificate, a *motu proprio* called *Tra Le Solicitudini*, that is, "Among the Concerns." This was a document on the renewal of sacred music. In it, the Holy Father states, "In order that the faithful may more actively participate in the sacred liturgy, let them be once again made to sing Gregorian Chant as a congregation."

So the term active participation means the restoration of Gregorian chant?

That's what the term "active participation" meant when it was first used in a papal document. But it had been used ten years earlier in another document, issued by Pius X before he was pope. He was the patriarch of Venice, and the document—as it turns out—was actually written by a Jesuit, with the wonderful name of Angelo de Santi ("angel of the saints"). In any case, the first use of *actuosa participatio*, i.e., active participation, referred explicitly and exclusively to the restoration of the congregational singing of Gregorian Chant. In 1928, Pope Pius XI reiterated the point in his Apostolic Letter, *Divini Cultus*. Nineteen years after that, in the *Magna Carta* of liturgical reform, *Mediator Dei*, issued by Pius XII, the same term was used with the same meaning. **So, until the Second Vatican Council, the term "active participation" referred exclusively to the singing of Gregorian Chant by the people.**

What was the primary aim of the liturgical renewal?

So the Council itself defines the primary aim of liturgical renewal: full, conscious, and active participation. How does the Council initially intend for the aim to be achieved? That, also, is not something we have to guess at or speculate on: "And, therefore, pastors of souls must zealously strive to achieve it by means of the necessary instruction in all their pastoral work." The Council's idea is clear: the liturgy is to be renewed by promoting more active participation through the means of greater education.

Did the Council call for all these innovations that we see at the New Order of the Mass?

Nothing whatsoever is said here about any kind of changes or reform of the rite itself. Later, when changes are discussed, the Council states in paragraph 23: "There must be no innovations unless the good of the Church genuinely and certainly requires them." So no changes unless there is a real, proven, demonstrable need. Paragraph 23 continues: "And care must be taken that any new forms adopted should in some way grow organically from forms already existing." Organic growth—like a plant, a flower, a tree—not something constructed by an intellectual elite, not things fabricated and tacked on.

What specific paragraph talks about the Mass in Sacrosanctum Concilium?

Paragraph 48 begins the chapter on the Mass. And the title of this chapter is interesting. It's not called "The Eucharist" or "The Mass"; it's called "The Most Sacred Mystery of the Eucharist." Even in the chapter title, you have the sense that what's important is mystery, sacredness, awe, the transcendence of God.

Did Sacrosanctum Concilium want lay Catholics to have a greater knowledge and awareness of "Holy Mass"?

Paragraph 48 returns to the theme of greater awareness, a greater knowledge of the faithful, in order that they might enter more fully into the mysteries celebrated: "For this reason the Church, therefore, earnestly desires that Christ's faithful, when present at the mystery of faith should not be there as strangers or silent spectators. On the contrary, through a good understanding of the rites and prayers, they should take part in the sacred action conscious of what they are doing with devotion and full collaboration."

When did the liturgical renewal start being discussed in the Church?

Paragraphs 50 to 58 of *Sacrosanctum Concilium* contain nine specific changes the Council had in mind for the renewal of the liturgy. But before we consider them, we must recall that when the Council made these proposals, it didn't dream them up overnight. Although this was the first document issued at the Council, it was not issued without long preparation. The modern liturgical movement began in the middle of the 19th century. It was given great impetus by Pius X himself, in the beginning of the 20th century, and by years of study, prayer, and liturgical congresses during the first half of the century. In fact, after *Mediator Dei* in 1947, there were seven international liturgical conferences, attended by liturgical experts, by pastors and by Roman officials. If you read the minutes of those meetings and the concrete proposals they made, you will see that what the Council outlines here is the fruit of those meetings. This is really the distillation of the prayer and reflection that was the culmination of the liturgical movement, which had existed for over a century prior to the Council.

What are the nine liturgical proposals made by Vatican II's Sacrosanctum Concilium?

The nine liturgical proposals, or the nine liturgical mandates, of the Council:

I.   **Paragraph 50 says the rites are to be simplified and those things that have been**

duplicated with the passage of time or added with little advantage, are to be discarded. And, after the Council, this reform did take place in many ways. I think it took place to a much greater degree than the Council intended, but there are certain simplifications in the Mass that the Council clearly intended.

II. Paragraph 51: The treasures of the Bible are to be opened up more fully. That has been accomplished by a greater number of readings from the Bible interspersed throughout the liturgical cycle, both in the Sunday and weekday cycles. Now, especially if you attend daily Mass, you have a much richer fare, if you will — a much expanded selection of Biblical readings.

III. Paragraph 52 says: "The homily is to be highly esteemed as part of the Liturgy itself." The Council called for a greater effort to have good homilies and I think the effort has been made. Whether the homilies are better or not, you can judge for yourselves.

[Fr. Fessio is an exception, but, generally speaking, the homilies at the average parish where we have the NOM are horizontal, with an emphasis on liberation social justice, not judging anyone, focusing only on God's love and mercy to the exclusion of His justice and awe-fullness, highlighting that all are welcome and that we are a community. They rarely speak about the devil, never speak about Hell, and never speak about sins against the sixth and ninth commandments. They throw in a few jokes here, a few jokes there, and then encourage everyone to go meet in the hall for some coffee and doughnuts. I have noticed that the homilies at the TLM are often rooted in such hard-hitting material as Thomistic philosophy, and there is a heavy emphasis on the lives of the saints, constant references to the early Church Fathers and Doctors of the Church. The biblical stories are taken seriously. I walk out and feel like I deserve three college units after the LM homilies. If you want to hear a typical homily from a TLM priest, visit the online outlet Sensus Fidelium, and your knowledge of the Catholic Faith will be stretched, while your intellect is stimulated and your will strengthened.]

IV. Paragraph 53 says that the Common Prayer or Prayer of the Faithful should be restored, and that's been done, too.

V. Paragraph 54 is a key paragraph: **"In Masses which are celebrated with the people, a suitable place may be allotted to their mother tongue."** What did the Council have in mind? Let's continue: "This is to apply in the first place, to the readings and to the Common Prayer. But also, as local conditions may warrant, to those parts which pertain to the people." Yet it goes on to say, "Nevertheless steps should be taken so that the faithful may also be able to say or to sing together in Latin those parts of the Ordinary of the Mass"—(that is, the unchanging parts, the parts that are there every day)—"which pertain to them."

So, the Council did not abolish Latin in the liturgy. The Council permitted the vernacular in certain limited ways, but clearly understood that the fixed parts of the Mass would remain in Latin. Again, I am just telling you what the Council said.

VI. Paragraph 55 discusses receiving Communion, if possible, from hosts consecrated at the Mass in which you participate. That is often done or attempted in many parishes today, but it is difficult to do in a precise way. It's hard to calculate the exact number of hosts you will need. Also, you have to keep some hosts in the Tabernacle for the sick and for adoration. **The Council also permits Communion under both species here, but under very limited circumstances.** For example, "to the newly ordained in the Mass of the Sacred Ordination, or the newly professed in the Mass of Profession, and the newly baptized in the Mass which follows baptism." **The Council itself did not call for offering both species to all the**

faithful all the time, but it did grant limited permission for it.

VII. Paragraph 56 says that there are two parts of the Liturgy, the Word and the Eucharist, and that a pastor should insistently teach the faithful to take part in the entire Mass, especially on Sundays and Feasts of Obligation. That is, to consider the first part of the Mass, the Table of the Word, as a significant and essential part of the Mass, so you don't think you have gone to Mass just by coming after the Offertory and being there for the Consecration and Communion.

VIII. Paragraph 57 states that concelebration should be permitted.

IX. Paragraph 58, that a new rite for concelebration is to be drawn up.

That is the sum total of the nine mandates of the Council for change in the ritual itself.

Are there other pertinent paragraphs worth mentioning from Sacrosanctum Concilium?

In paragraph 112, in which the Council speaks specifically of music, we read: "The musical tradition of the Universal Church is a treasure of inestimable value, greater even than that of any other art." That is a stupendous and shocking statement; the Council actually says that the Church's music is a treasure of art greater than any other treasure of art she has. Think about that. Think about Chartres Cathedral. Think about the *Pieta*. Think about Da Vinci's *Last Supper*. Think of all the crucifixes from Catalonia in Spain, and all the Church architecture and art and paintings and sculpture. **The Council boldly says that the Church's musical tradition is a treasure of inestimable value greater than any other art.**

[We have talked a lot about sacred music and its opposite, but, in light of what Fr. Fessio has pointed out here, I'll ask again: How did we go from authentic sacred music, the greatest artistic treasure of our Church, to the insipid, foot-tapping, hand-clapping, folksy pop music at your average parish? How did our liturgical music go off the rails like it has? I will answer my question: The modernists, with their false notion of ecumenism and their aversion to Latin, have given us the most banal liturgical music in two thousand years. I would far prefer a silent Mass over what I have heard in the average parish.]

Why did Sacrosanctum Concilium *emphasize sacred music?*

"The main reason for this preeminence is that, as sacred song united to the words, it forms a necessary or integral part of the solemn liturgy." What that means is this: it's wonderful to have a beautiful church, stained glass windows, statues, a noble crucifix, prayerful architecture that lift your heart up to God. But those are all surroundings of the Mass. It's the "worship environment," as they would say today. But it's not the Mass itself. **The Council says that when the Mass itself is set to music, that's what ennobles music, which, itself, enhances the Mass; and that's what makes the musical tradition the most precious tradition of the Church.**

Are the hymns we sing in our parishes what Vatican II called for?

The Council implies what many Church documents have said explicitly—that the most perfect form of music at Mass is not the hymns, the so-called "Gathering hymn" and its antithesis—I guess you would call it the "Scattering hymn"—at the end. **The most appropriate use of music at Mass, as seen by Church tradition and reaffirmed by the Council, is singing the Mass itself: the *Kyrie*, the *Agnus Dei*, the *Sanctus*, the *Acclamations*, the *Alleluias*** and so on. Again, this isn't Father Fessio's pet theory; this is what the Council actually says. Paragraph 112 adds, "Sacred music is to be considered the more holy in proportion as it is the more closely connected with the liturgical action itself." This reinforces my point.... Paragraph 114 adds: "The treasure of sacred music is to be preserved and fostered with great care." **Then in paragraph 116 we find another shocker: "The Church acknowledges Gregorian Chant as especially suited to the Roman Liturgy. Therefore, other things being equal, it should be given pride of place in liturgical services."** That's what the Council actually said. If you are in a parish which prides itself on living the spirit of Vatican II, then you should be singing Gregorian chant at your parish. And if you're not singing the Gregorian Chant, you're not following the specific mandate of the Second Vatican Council.

Where did Catholics get Gregorian chant? Where did it originate?

Just a little footnote on the Gregorian Chant. In reflecting on these things about Church music, I began to think about the Psalms a few years back. And a very obvious idea suddenly struck me. Why it didn't come earlier I don't know, but the fact is that the Psalms are songs. Every one of the 150 Psalms is meant to be sung; and was sung by the Jews. When this thought came to me, I immediately called a friend, a rabbi in San Francisco who runs the Hebrew School, and I asked, "Do you sing the Psalms at your synagogue?" "Well, no, we recite them," he said. "Do you know what they sounded like when they were sung in the Old Testament times and the time of Jesus and the Apostles?" I asked. He said, "No, but why don't you call this company in Upstate New York. They publish Hebrew music, and they may know." So, I called the company and they said, "We don't know; call 1-800-JUDAISM." So I did. And I got an information center for Jewish traditions, and they didn't know either. But they said, "You call this music teacher in Manhattan. He will know." So, I called this wonderful rabbi in Manhattan and we had a long conversation. **At the end, I said, "I want to bring some focus to this, can you give me any idea what it sounded like when Jesus and his Apostles sang the Psalms?" He said, "Of course, Father. It sounded like Gregorian Chant. You got it from us."**

I was amazed. I called Professor William Mahrt, a Professor of Music at Stanford University and a friend. I said, "Bill, is this true?" He said, "Yes. The Psalm tones have their roots in ancient Jewish hymnody and psalmody." So, you know something? If you sing the Psalms at Mass with the Gregorian tones, you are as close as you can get to praying with Jesus and Mary. They sang the Psalms in tones that have come down to us today in Gregorian Chant.

Some liturgical, modernist, liberal Catholics say that Gregorian chant takes us back to those horrible Middle Ages. Your thoughts?

So, the Council isn't calling us back to some medieval practice, those "horrible" medieval times, the "terrible" Middle Ages, when they knew so little about liturgy that all they could do was build a Chartres Cathedral. (When I see cathedrals and churches built that have a tenth of the beauty of Notre Dame de Paris, then I will say that the liturgists have the right to speak. Until then, they have no right to speak about beauty in the liturgy.) **But my point is that at the time of Notre Dame de Paris in the 13th century, the Psalms tones were already over a thousand years old. They are called "Gregorian" after Pope Gregory I, who reigned from 590 to 604. But they were already a thousand years old when he reigned. He didn't invent Gregorian chant; he reorganized and codified it and helped to establish musical schools to sing it and teach it. It was a reform; it wasn't an invention. Thus, the Council really calls us back to an unbroken tradition of truly sacred music and gives such music pride of place.**

What about sacred art and sacred furnishings? Did Vatican II give us any direction or instruction?

I want to quote from the Council ... paragraph 128, which talks about sacred art and sacred furnishings: "Along with the revisions of liturgical books ... there is to be an earlier revision of the canons and ecclesiastical statutes which govern the provisions of material things involved in sacred worship. These laws refer especially to the worthy and well-planned construction of sacred buildings, the shape and construction of altars, the nobility, placing and safety of the Eucharistic tabernacle, the dignity and suitability of the baptistery ..." and so on.

So what did the Council not say?

That's essentially what the Second Vatican Council actually said about the renewal of the liturgy. Let me tell you what it did not say. The Council did not say that tabernacles should be moved from their central location to some other location. In fact, it specifically said we should be concerned about the worthy and dignified placing of the tabernacle. The Council did not say that Mass should be celebrated facing the people. That is not in Vatican II; it is not mentioned. It is not even raised in the documents that record the formation of the Constitution on the Liturgy; it didn't come up. Mass facing the people is not a requirement of Vatican II; it is not in the spirit of Vatican II; it is definitely not in the letter of Vatican II. It is something introduced in 1969. **And, by the way, never in the history of the Church, East or West, was there a tradition of celebrating Mass facing the people. Never, ever, until 1969.**

What does Vatican II say about the priest facing ad orientem?

I can say without fear of contradiction from anyone who knows the facts that there is simply no tradition whatsoever, in the history of the Church, of Mass facing the people. Now, is it a sin? No. Is it wrong? No. Is it permitted? Yes. Is it required? Not at all. **In fact in the Latin Roman Missal, which is the typical edition that all the translations of the Missal are based on (not always translated properly, but at least based on it) the rubrics actually presuppose the Mass facing East, the Mass facing the Lord.**

Have you always celebrated the Holy Mass ad orientem?

For the first 25 years of my priesthood, I celebrated Mass like you see it when you go to a typical parish: in English, facing the people. It can be done reverently; I've seen it done reverently; I've tried to do it reverently myself. But ... after study and reflection, I've changed. I actually think the Mass facing the people is a mistake. But, even if it's not, at least this much we can say: **there is no** permission required to say Mass facing God, facing the taber-nacle, facing East, facing *with* the people. And it should be given equal rights, it seems to me, with Mass facing the people. It's been around for 1800 years at least, and it should be allowed to continue. I happen to think it's symbolically richer.

What is the temptation for a priest when he celebrates Holy Mass facing the people?

It's true that when the priest faces the people for the celebration of the Eucharistic Sacrifice, there may be a sense of greater unity as a community. But there is also a danger of the priest being the per-former and you being the spectator—precisely what the Council did not want: priest performers and congregational spectators. But there is something more problematic. You can see it, perhaps, by contrasting Mass facing the people with Mass facing East or facing the Lord. **I don't say Mass "with my back to the people" any more than Patton went through Germany with his "back to the soldiers." Patton led the Third Army across Germany and they followed him to achieve a goal. The Mass is part of the Pilgrim Church on the way to our goal, our heavenly homeland. This world is not our heavenly homeland. We don't sit around in a circle and look at each other. We want to look *with* each other and with the priest towards the rising sun, the rays of grace, where the Son will come again in glory on the clouds.**

Does the priest ever face the people in a NOM in which he is primarily ad orientem?

The priest does face the people when he speaks on God's behalf to proclaim the Word and explain it. And he does face the people when he receives their gifts. And then he turns to face with the people and to offer those gifts up to our common Father, praying that the Holy Spirit will come down and transform those gifts into the Body and Blood of Christ. And when that most sacred act takes place, the priest turns to offer the gifts back to the people. I think that is much more dramatic.... Now strange as it may appear, there is absolutely no permission required to say Mass facing East. The Pope (John Paul II) does it every morning in his chapel. But there is such a taboo against it that most pastors would be afraid to do it for fear they would be exiled to some lowly parish.

Did Vatican II say anything about removing the tabernacle from the center?

The Council ... said nothing about moving the Tabernacle. It said nothing about removing altar rails. It said nothing about taking out kneelers. It said nothing about turning the altar around. It said nothing about multiple canons. That, too, is an invention; a pure invention.

What one word describes the liturgists at Vatican II?

One problem, both at the time of the Council and after, is **rationalism**, which the Holy Father has spoken against. This is the idea that we can do it all with our own minds. The liturgists after the Council tried to construct a more perfect liturgy. But you know something? When you've grown up in a house and a room is added on and a story added on, a garage is added on, it may not be architecturally perfect, but it's your home. To destroy it and try to construct a new one out of steel and glass and tile because that's the modern idea, is not the way you live a human life. But that's what's happened to the liturgy.

How are the vernacular and Latin supposed to interrelate at Holy Mass?

The Council, as I mentioned, did not abolish Latin. It specifically mandated the retention of Latin and only permitted the use of the vernacular in certain circumstances. And, finally, the Council did not prohibit Gregorian Chant, as you might be led to think from its absence in your parishes. The Council actually prescribed Gregorian Chant to have pride of place.

Did Pope John Paul II ask for awe and reverence at the Vatican II Mass?

In 1998 all the bishops of the United States went to Rome for their *Ad Limina* visit.... It happened that when the bishops from the Northwest came from Alaska, Washington, Oregon, Montana and Idaho—the Holy Father spoke on the liturgy.... The Pope, here, speaks to our bishops, looking toward the new millennium and says, in effect: *Here is what I think is the plan God has for all of his people as we move to the next millennium. And, specifically, here is the liturgical blueprint that, I, the Holy Father, believe we are to follow.* "The challenge now," he continues, "is to move beyond whatever misunderstandings there have been and to reach the proper point of balance, especially by entering more deeply into the contemplative dimension of worship, which includes a sense of awe, reverence and adoration which are fundamental attitudes in our relationship with God." What does the Pope say we must do to restore balance? Enter more deeply into the contemplative dimension of worship. Can you contemplate when you've got drummers up in the sanctuary? Where do we find the sense of awe? Not in this "chatty" stuff at Mass: "*Good morning, everybody.*" Does that inspire a sense of awe? "Have a nice day." The Pope mentions reverence and adoration. Standing is a sign of respect; but kneeling is a sign of adoration. The Pope says we must restore the sense of adoration.

Did Pope John Paul II give priests the authority to invent or produce innovations in the liturgy?

This is why it's so important that liturgical law be respected, because an objective act is taking place. Pope John Paul II said: "The priest, who is the servant of the liturgy and not its inventor or producer, has a particular responsibility in this regard, lest he empty the liturgy of its true meaning or obscure its sacred character."

What did Pope John Paul II say about "full, conscious and active participation" as it relates to the NOM?

The Holy Father next discusses three attributes of the liturgy: full, conscious and active participation. First, he talks about the fullness of participation. "The sharing of all the baptized in the one priest-hood of Jesus Christ is the key to understanding the Church's call for full, conscious and active participation. Full participation certainly means that every member of the community has a part to play in the liturgy.... But, full participation does not mean that everyone does everything. Since this would lead to a clericalizing of the laity and a laicizing of the priesthood, and this was not what the Council had in mind."

What does Pope John Paul II mean by "clericalizing the laity"?

It's the idea that, for example, the lector, the server at the altar, or the cross-bearer participates more actively than the mother with her child in the back of church. It's the idea that being more like the priest in the sanctuary somehow makes you participate more fully. But the Pope says no to that idea. No, the "clericalizing of the laity" and the "laicizing of the clergy," whereby the priest doesn't do priestly things but sits while lay people are distributing the Eucharist, are not what the Council had in mind, says the Pope.

Does "active participation" at the NOM deny "contemplative adoration" according to Pope John Paul II?

The Pope (John Paul II) said: "Active participation certainly means that in gesture, word, song, and service all the members of the community take part in an active worship, which is anything but inert or passive. Yet active participation does not preclude the active passivity of silence, stillness, and listening: indeed, it demands it. Worshippers are not passive, for instance, when listening to the readings or the homily or following the prayers of the celebrant and the chants in music of the Liturgy. These are experiences of silence and stillness, but they are in their own way, profoundly active. In a culture that neither favors nor fosters meditative quiet, the art of interior listening is learned only with difficulty. Here we see the liturgy, though it must always be properly inculturated, must also be counter-cultural."

Fr. Fessio, can you add anything else to what Pope John Paul II has said?

Especially in our noisy world, we need to have silence. Especially in our world where it is hard to pray, we need to have contemplative adoration. Conscious participation, then, is not a multiplication of commentators telling us what's happening as the Mass goes along; it's not laid back informality and the trivializing of the liturgy. That's why I think it may seem like a small thing, but it's a very bad thing to begin a liturgy by saying, "Good morning, everyone."

That's not how you begin a *sacred* liturgy. You begin a *sacred* liturgy, "In the Name of the Father, and of the Son, and of the Holy Spirit," or better yet, "*In nomine Patris, et Filii, et Spiritus Sancti.*"

Can you describe the three ways that Holy Mass is celebrated today post–Vatican II?

We have now two extremes and a moderate position. One extreme position is the kind of informal Mass, all in English, facing the people, with contemporary music, which does not at all correspond with what the Council had in mind. But it is legitimate, it is permitted; it is not wrong. **And we have on the other extreme those who have returned, with permission, to the Mass of 1962 and, as others have noted, it is thriving and growing. But it is not what the Council itself specifically had in mind, although it is the Mass of the ages.** Then you have the moderates. Those in the middle. Me and a few others. But I am going to insist on my right as a Catholic and as priest to celebrate the liturgy according to the Council, according to the presently approved liturgical books, to celebrate a form of the Mass that therefore needs no special permission — and which in fact cannot be prohibited — what I've called "the Mass of Vatican II."

CHAPTER 8

"SACROSANCTUM CONCILIUM: A LAWYER EXAMINES THE LOOPHOLES" BY LAWYER CHRISTOPHER FERRARA[60]

Does Sacrosanctum Concilium *give liturgists a blank check for creating a new liturgy?*

No one who reads *SC* carefully in the light of our experience since the Council can deny that it constitutes a "blank check" for liturgical reform, with the amount to be filled in depending entirely upon who is wielding the pen. The few "conservative" norms which seem to limit the possibility of liturgical change are clearly overwhelmed by the far more numerous and pervasive "liberal" norms which create an almost unlimited potential for destruction of the liturgy.

Does Sacrosanctum Concilium *specify a change in the text or rubrics of the traditional order of the Mass?*

Except for restoring the prayer of the faithful in Article 53, *SC* does not actually *mandate a single specific change in the text or rubrics of*

---

[60] Christopher Ferrara, "*Sacrosanctum Concilium*: A Lawyer Examines the Loopholes," Free Republic, August 25, 2003, https://freerepublic.com/focus/f-religion/970035/posts. Christopher Ferrara is the founder of *Catholic Family News*, a traditionalist Catholic monthly publication of Catholic Family Ministries.

the traditional Order of Mass. This would appear to be the main reason the Council Fathers were induced to vote for the document, since it did not threaten any apparent harm to the Latin liturgical tradition. And it is also the reason neither the "conservatives" nor anyone else can determine "the authentic reform desired by the Council" from a reading of *SC.*

Did Sacrosanctum Concilium mandate any particular reforms? Who did the reforming?

While *SC* opened the way to all manner of possible liturgical reforms, the simple truth of the matter is that it *mandated no particular reform of the liturgy. SC* is, quite simply, silent about what kind of reformed liturgy the Council Fathers had in mind, if indeed the Council majority shared any common conception at all about the matter. In practice, however, *SC* unquestionably served as the license for a vast project of liturgical reform and the ceding of effective control over the liturgy to the national hierarchies, with calamitous results.

What is the solution to the liturgical confusion that we find ourselves in? What do you think should be done to bring liturgical uniformity and reverence back?

The emergence of "conservative" demands for an "authentic reform" of the liturgy demonstrate that unless *SC* is reconsidered, along with the disastrous changes it engendered, the liturgical crisis in the Roman Rite will never end. The demands for "renewal" by liberals on the one hand, and for "authentic renewal" by conservatives on the other, will continue to revolve around this utterly problematical document so long as it continues to serve as a warrant for the liturgical-reformist mentality, which the Council unwittingly unleashed upon the Church.

The only way to restrain that mentality and restore liturgical sanity in the Roman Rite is *full restoration of our Latin liturgical tradition*—taken from us overnight [after Vatican II].

CHAPTER 9

"BISHOP'S CHALLENGE" BY FR. DONALD KLOSTER[61]

18 February 2024
To the Catholic Bishops:

THE TRUTH OF OUR much lamented position as the Church is in the sacramental records. This is specifically found in the change of the priest to faithful ratio over the last fifty-four years. This ratio is as telling as it gets. Obviously, the lower the priest to faithful ratio, the more the Mystical Body of Christ is served. The larger the ratio, the harder it becomes for the faithful to go to Mass, have their Confessions heard, or to have a meaningful contact with priests at all.

In 1970, the year that the Novus Ordo Mass was introduced, we had 59,192 USA priests and around 52 million Catholics or about 1:881. Today we have around 28,000 priests and 72 million Catholics or about 1:2,571. We have one-third the priests that we had right after the unexpected innovation of the Novus Ordo Mass. In the five plus decades since 1970, the ratio of priests to faithful has never gotten better; it keeps cratering.

---

[61] Donald Kloster "Bishop's Challenge," in Return to Tradition, May 05, 2024, https://returntotradition.org/priest-publicly-challenges-bishops-to-defend-sacred-tradition/.

The Catholic Church is in dire straits. In the 1950's we had approximately eighty percent of our Catholics attending Sunday Mass. In 1980, it was about fifty percent. By 1990, it was around forty percent, and by 2000 it was about thirty-three percent. By 2019, it had fallen to twenty percent. Currently, a Diocese is fortunate to count eight percent of those who identify as Catholics, attending Sunday Mass. No company lets its main product keep tanking year to year much less decade over decade. The Bishops, as stewards of the Holy Faith, should intuitively reevaluate the consequences of the changes in the Holy Mass. There have been two important studies on the Traditional Latin Mass (2019 and 2020). These TLM faithful live in the exact same society as their Novus Ordo Mass fellow Catholics. The falling numbers in all things Catholic Church related, are not due to the societal moral and theological rot. The TLM faithful go to Mass at a ninety-seven percent clip and give five times more money per capita. These figures were reviewed and verified by Dr. Froehle who ran CARA, a national church research center at Georgetown University, for many years. You, as Bishops, can't say anymore that no one wants the TLM. That's what we heard time and again when I was in the seminary in the early 1990's. Not only do people want the TLM, they know it is the lone protective cover from the assaults of Satan. Every other religious practice is being demolished. Practicing Christians or any modern religion, is ceding to a non-practice and/or a type of atheistic godlessness. To me, it is nefarious to insinuate that the Novus Ordo Mass can even exist in the future. The Novus Ordo Mass is stuck in a 1960's time warp. It neither resembles our Traditional Liturgy nor does it remotely approach any Eternal reality test.

Some Bishops believe that an oriented Novus Ordo in Latin is the answer. They want to coax or massage a belief that the

Novus Ordo Mass in Latin will satiate the TLM faithful; not so as it is spiritually a far weaker imitation. The problem is that this idea has already been tried and failed. I will say that the Novus Ordo in Latin is far better than the Novus Ordo in the Vernacular. However, it will just be a slower bleed. The Novus Ordo Mass in Latin has no upside growth, no vocations increase. It is still a breach of an over 1,930 year Holy Mass, from the Apostles, tradition.

Why on earth would a Catholic Prelate allow growing Traditional Latin Masses in his Diocese to be canceled? What harm have these people done? Do they give too much to the collection? Do they get married too often? Do they come to Sunday Masses too regularly? Do they have too many Catholic children because they are not practicing contraception? We know that eighty-nine percent of normal NOM attending women agree with contraception and only two percent of TLM women agree with contraception. The overarching contraception mentality in the Novus Ordo speaks volumes as to the atrophy it engenders. These Masses seem to produce two different religions.

A sitting Prelate of the Catholic Church is not a Vicar of Rome. He is the authority in his Dioceses for his faithful. He is the one who should decide what is spiritually beneficial for his faithful. Are almost all of you afraid of the Roman Curia? If you are removed like Bishop Strickland, so be it. St. Thomas Aquinas teaches that obedience to tyrannical demands is not tenable. If enough Bishops resist, they have great power staying united together in a group of virtuous stalwarts. In 16th Century England, only one Bishop out of thirty resisted King Henry VIII. St. John Fisher stood up for marriage and the Latin Mass of the Ages. In 1569, the Nobles of Northumberland fought against Queen Elizabeth I in favor of the Traditional Latin Mass and against the English Anglican Liturgy.

Our exorcists are repeatedly telling us that the demons hate and fear Latin. I would hope you all would neither be a willing nor negligent accomplice to the powers of Hell. Many faithful have run their own businesses for years. They would never deny their customers their best-selling product! That would be economic suicide. Seeing the TLMs around the country being arbitrarily shut down looks like spiritual suicide to me. Do you, as a Bishop, want to spend the final years of your Episcopacy presiding over the continued hemorrhaging of our faithful? Do you listen to your faithful who love the TLM and its history of fruitfulness? Do you have eyes to see and ears to hear? Are we the only segment of the Church that gets no paternal affection and care? The fruitfulness of any Mass should attest to its veracity or mendacity.

The vocations to the priesthood in TLM parishes is 6-7 times greater depending on the Diocese. To date, I have been assigned in five parishes that offered both Masses on the same Sunday schedule. The Novus Ordo Mass had exponentially far more attendees than the Traditional Latin Mass at every parish. The vocations results were 15 TLM to 0 NOM. In my twenty-eight years as a priest, I have had twenty-nine Spiritual Directees who have discerned the Priesthood or the Religious Life. Twenty-eight TLM and one NOM. Seven of the TLM left formation before their final vows or ordinations. The one NOM was ordained a priest and then left the Priesthood. So it's 21 TLM to 0 NOM still continuing in their formation or vows.

Please, any Bishop reading this; prove to me that I am wrong about the negative growth of the NOM and the positive growth of the TLM where it is not indiscriminately smashed. Let them stand side by side. Let the faithful decide. Please stop aiding anyone, perhaps you yourself, who is putting his finger on the scale to his own benefit. There should be no place for Egoism (Bishops who are jealous of the success of the TLM), no place for an Experimental Mass that has not worked, no place for the Effeminacy (the feminine Liturgy of the NOM as opposed to the masculine Liturgy of the TLM) that has undermined the Son of Man Incarnate on the Altar.

Why does it appear that the lone fruitful sector of the Church is being ignored? I once heard a man say that he didn't care if the priest spoke Martian as long as the Holy Faith was bolstered. The Latin Rite is the name of our Western Church. Latin reverses the curse of the Tower of Babel. It gives us one universal language. It seems to me that we need more unity, not the squelching of the Spirit of our forefathers.

Part III

Introduction: Men Share What the TLM Means for Them

For this last section of my book—a book that I wrote for men so that they could see how the TLM is their natural and supernatural home on this earth—I reached out to eight of my friends whom I know to be authentic Catholic men. In these short chapters, I asked them to share what the TLM has done for them, what it means to them, and why they are hooked on it.

These men come from a wide variety of walks of life, all of them totally hard-core. Most are laymen, but one priest, Fr. Craig Friedley, also provided his testimonial. Before he was a priest, he was a fighter pilot for the U.S. Air Force, flying F-111s and F-16s. Charlie Aeschliman is a former Navy SEAL, Eddie Brock is a former U.S. Marine and a police officer, Harrison Butker is an NFL star who's won three Super Bowls, Kyle Clement is a rancher and assistant to an exorcist, Bas Rutten is a UFC champion, Dan Schneider is a theology professor at Franciscan University of Steubenville—and a veteran of the Gulf War and former Cobra helicopter pilot for the U.S. Army—and Scott Sullivan is a heavyweight kickboxing champ and martial arts instructor.

All of these men know what it is to train themselves physically, to discipline themselves mentally and spiritually, and how to prioritize God among their many skills and dedications. In their quest for authentic masculinity and the authentic practice of the Catholic Faith, they have all come to the TLM. It is here that they have found the liturgy that calls them out of themselves and enables them to approach and encounter the Divine in a way that is unlike anything else on this earth.

Many thanks to all of these excellent men for sharing their stories.

CHAPTER 10

CHARLIE AESCHLIMAN

THE NAVY SEALS ARE tasked with some of the military's toughest top secret missions. At a moment's notice they must be ready to engage in dangerous military operations in the sea, from the air, or on the land. As a former Navy SEAL, I was honored to be a part of this team, fighting for freedom.

Being a Catholic is also a call to arms and to engaging in battle: spiritual warfare! Every Catholic is called to put on the armor of God, join the fight, and save the world with Jesus Christ. To carry out his duties, each Navy SEAL is equipped with an incredible arsenal of special weapons, tactics, and armaments to defeat the enemy. The Catholic Church also provides her members with an awesome array of arms: spiritual weapons. Granted, the weapons and tactics of the commando may differ from those of the Catholic, but the intensity of the spiritual battle and the consequences are just as real and cannot be taken lightly. After all, this is a battle for the eternal destiny of our souls and the conversion of the world.

Men have been called by God to lead the charge toward Heaven and the fight against the evils that stand in the way of salvation. For ourselves, our families, and all of mankind. This is why I find the recent calls from the Vatican to "demasculinize" the Church, along with further restrictions being placed on the Traditional Latin Mass, troubling. These calls seem to be counterproductive because, by our

God-given nature, men are called to be protectors, providers, and spiritual leaders. It's in our DNA.

Instead of calls to demasculinize the Church, we need a clarion call for a "few good men." Actually, we need an army of good men! If Christ's Church is to sanctify society as He commanded, then it is men who must carry His banner of faith, hope, and love into the battle against evil. And so the Church needs to attract men and to encourage and promote their virtues of manliness within her liturgies. Men should be fed, strengthened, and inspired. Men's souls need to be bolstered and rallied to go out and lead the charge to "take that hill" and to establish our Lord's shining city of light on top for the world to see.

I believe attendance at the Traditional Latin Mass provides that source of strength and rallying point for men's souls. The TLM is a remedy for the Church's problems; it is not one of her ills. It has a natural attraction for men because, within its beautiful and majestic nature, it has an inherently masculine appeal.

The TLM has an intriguing sense of mystery that draws you into it. The reverence and sacredness by which it is celebrated tells our souls that we are worshipping and serving something greater than ourselves. This *inspires* men! The sound and cadence of the spoken Latin gives it a unique, unfamiliar, and ancient feel. The Gregorian chant is dignified and masculine, not modern and trite. This appeals to men! The rubrics and actions of the priest are precise, purposeful, and conducted with a sense of seriousness, like that of a determined, disciplined soldier. This attracts men!

You get the sense that something of incredible magnitude is happening here. It inspires an awe and deeper devotion to the one whose sacrifice is being made present on the altar. And along with the vestments, incense, altar cloths, and candles, our senses are transported and lifted up to the heavens. Indeed, the Mass of the

Ages is "Heaven brought to earth." This moves and motivates men to answer Christ's call to pick up His Cross and follow in His footsteps!

As men, we need a cause. Something to fight for, to believe in. Like I said, I had the privilege to serve our country as a Navy SEAL, but what a greater honor you have as a Catholic man to serve our Lord Jesus Christ! To stand in the ranks of His mighty Church Militant. Fighting for good and battling evil by bringing the light and love of our Lord to a dark and desperate world. Indeed, we need a few good men. Are you one of them?

CHAPTER 11

EDDIE BROCK

I WAS RAISED IN a single-parent African American home in West Philadelphia, in the '70s and '80s. I attended Catholic schools all my life, except my senior year of high school. During those times in Philly, I attended the NOM everywhere I went to Mass. I never participated in the TLM. My mom often referred to times when she was a young girl and was taught to pray the Mass in Latin. Clearly, I did not know what she was talking about, nor did I ask.

After high school, I entered the Marine Corps because I wanted to be a part of the finest fighting organization America had to offer. As a kid, I was intoxicated when I saw the precision of the purposeful movements of Marines and upon hearing countless stories of heroism in battle and war. I wanted in on that form of masculinity!

I left the Corps after Desert Shield/Desert Storm, and I joined local law enforcement in Southern California, where I am still a contributing member. Law enforcement has filled in some of the innate needs I seem to have for helping people. Leading men in service of others is the greatest employment one can have, bar none!

About three years ago, I completed a course titled Church History, and, from our readings, I learned of the Extraordinary Form of the Mass. Once I learned about it, I switched to attending Mass in this glorious form, and I have never looked back.

Attending my first few Masses in the Extraordinary Form was very difficult, but I could not tear myself away from the mysterious and beautiful things I witnessed. During Mass, I didn't understand any of the prayers in Latin; I could recognize only our Lord's coming and being offered for mankind on the altar. Learning Latin and all I could about this form of the Mass consumed me. It was difficult and arduous, similar to some of the missions I have experienced in my service careers. Unlike the life-and-death difficulties I sometimes faced at work, the life and death celebrated at the TLM leaves no question about the eternal benefits for those who participate. Witnessing it all in this form seems to connect me to the richness of the language, movements, vestments, smells, and sounds of the past, here and now. Everything appears to have and does have a well-defined purpose, and everything complements everything else seamlessly within the simplicity and boldness of silence.

Praying the Mass within this mysterious form provides a definitive assurance for me that I am a man of God. In other words, I feel secure in my manhood while worshipping God and witnessing the Paschal Sacrifice. I equate attending the TLM with taking a short respite during a mission; we adjust our gear, tend to our needs, check our orientation, and march on to our target. As an altar server, the privilege to process up the aisle to the foot of the altar and assist the priest, an *alter Christus*, as he offers the Mass, is rivaled by no other experience in life.

My experiences at the foot of the altar during Mass have affirmed that men need order, ritual, and the fraternity that flows from this form of the Mass. The timeless and mysterious movements and rubrics of the Mass call for all men to come closer to investigate, to inquire what the Mass has to say. This is not a curiosity for useless satisfaction. This is one I've experienced, as I suspect most men have, to investigate, to explore deeper. As a patrolman rolls through his beat, ever vigilant for something out of place or looking to answer the call of the radio, one must patrol the annals of his life to see where witnessing the Paschal Mystery leads him. This mission must be accepted by all men because there is something there for us. Mysteries are things we can know about, albeit in a limited fashion, but in due time, through God's providence, we will come to know all we need to know. This particular mystery — celebrating the unbloodied sacrifice here in time — is a call to men to pray and witness as we continue our particular journey along the narrow path of life. We all have the mettle to be this man. Few will answer, although all are called to manhood via the crucible of faith. Here in the Extraordinary Form, we burn away the chaff and the straw of senseless music, tambourines, and busybodies milling around the sanctuary. As men, we humbly come to pray the Mass, and we lead our families in this great and noble prayer until we are called for our particular judgment.

I led men in the U.S. Marine Corps, and I served our nation faithfully. I lead men and women as chief of police, and I am currently serving as a law enforcement executive. Through all of the ups and downs of my work life, I've had a fantastic life providing for my family. Undoubtedly, I have never received a more important mission than that of providing for the souls I am responsible for: those of my wife and two children. This mission, with all the divine assistance of the angels and saints, is realized for me at every single Mass I pray. I encourage all men to take some part of my perspective and incorporate it into your op plan. Whatever your style, whatever route you take, I pray you are girded by the Extraordinary Form of the Mass.

Our worship here on earth, in union with all of Heaven, is the mission I am set on accomplishing in this lifetime. This reality, which still remains a mystery, is to be joined and lived by us faithful here on earth until all is made known to us in Heaven. I will faithfully maintain the lead of my family and myself and "show myself a man" (1 Kings 2:2) according to the dictate of King David to a young Solomon.

Blessed be God forever!

CHAPTER 12

HARRISON BUTKER

SINCE THE BEGINNING OF human existence, boys in particular have had an intense eagerness for finding role models. These role models tend to lay the foundation for their development into manhood. In our modern age, musicians, athletes, and movie stars (to name a few) often act as role models for boys. However, it is more ideal that the man of the house—the father—should serve in that role for their sons. A father should reflect the sacrificial love that our Lord so beautifully showed during His time on the earth. Just as the father in the home should be a role model, it is our spiritual fathers—our priests—who should be our constant role models, even beyond adolescence. When I attended my first Traditional Latin Mass, I was inspired by the priest. He followed the Missal, saying the black text and performing the actions written in red. He didn't have to make decisions about what parts to say or not to say or what actions to perform or not to perform. There was this beautiful obedience to the rich history of the liturgy. I saw this in the example of the celebrant as well as the sacred ministers and even in the example of the altar boys. I witnessed a dying to self that didn't allow for the individual to take over the Mass, that didn't allow an individual to make his own personality become the focal point.

Being fed by these powerful examples in the Traditional Latin Mass, I was pushed to humbly embrace the difficult and counter-cultural silence that is found only in the old Mass and to use it for my own deeper encounter with our Lord. As a fallen man, I am in constant need of these examples of sacrifice to self. Our spiritual fathers, in their example on the altar, should be constantly reminding us that everything we do, no matter how small, should be for His glory and not our own. Christ should always be the focal point, and this can happen only if we truly die to self.

I am so blessed to have access to the Traditional Latin Mass, and I am very thankful for the countless holy priests who embrace their vocation as the spiritual role models of the faithful, sacrificing so much to make this ancient treasure available to their flock.

KYLE CLEMENT

PART OF THE MASCULINE disposition is a desire for ritual and fraternity — *ritual* meaning order. Every man will tell you he has a ritual or a certain order of doing things, even down to the way he shaves or ties his shoes or dresses in the morning. It is this understanding of order — in the ordering of our mind — that we order our thoughts, words, and deeds. Oftentimes, when the interior is in tumult, we can restore order through the imposition of the exterior disciplines and movements of order requisite with our daily routine.

The Holy Roman Mass in the Tridentine Form is ordered, and it is order that lifts the soul toward Heaven. It is an unprecedented beauty being defined as that which is true and good. In the Traditional Latin Mass, we are truly *ad orientem*: creature focused on Creator, not creature focused on creature.

We understand, as men, both the implicit and the inferred leadership of the priest in the Traditional Latin Mass facing the altar of sacrifice. It is the ranking of his attention, as St. Thomas would say; the primacy of his attention is focused on the Holy Sacrifice of the Mass. We understand, as men, that we are configured to God through sacrifice — not through banquet, not through feast.

The banquet theology language, which diminished the Holy Sacrifice of the Mass, is indicative of the modernist/relativist bent that emphasizes the individual to the diminution, or even outright exclusion, of God. The Traditional Latin Mass keeps us forever focused on that which is actually important—namely, God Himself. One of the aspects of right-ordered masculinity is that singular focus on God, to the exclusion of all else.

Focus on God is best achieved in the Holy Sacrifice of the Mass in this traditional form. We, as men, find ourselves between the souls for whom we are responsible at our back and the world at large. We fight for what is behind us, while in front of us is a howling wasteland devoid of the landmarks of virtue, goodness, integrity, honesty—and any clear masculine leadership in the Church.

We are hesitant to lead these souls in our care into these ranges, into these grasslands and areas that are unknown. We don't know the plants, except inasmuch as it's clear that they have no nutritional value. They are full of puff and fluff but nothing substantial. They appeal to the emotion, but not to the intellect. And we stand with our feet on the edge of this wasteland, our arms outstretched, holding back these souls in our care, that they do not follow these effeminate, homosexual leaders into areas of spiritual peril, even though they claim to be new theology, new revelation.

It's quicksand. It's nothing nutritious. It's arid. It's barren. And it is devoid of the glory, laud, and honor due to our Lord.

I am drawn to the reality of the Holy Sacrifice of the Mass. I do not want wailing women, children, and disjointed liturgy when my bones are committed to the ground. I want the Requiem Mass with a priest who stands ramrod straight offering the Holy Sacrifice of the Mass, incensing so that my soul may rise, hopefully, to the judgment of mercy, and I want to hear the *Dies Irae*.

I want to live and die a Catholic, to live and die with clear purpose, to live and die offering the Holy Sacrifice to God in a truly extraordinary form.

I have been fortunate to have lived a very physical life. Together with my beautiful wife of forty-three years, I ranch for a living. All I ever wanted was to be a cowboy, and my heroes were my father, my grandfathers, and my uncles: silent men who knew subtlety, who knew the ability to communicate with a glance, who knew what it was not only to be a man but to make a man. And that is done through order day to day, but done first through right relationship with God. Our family is surrounded by order in breeding, gestation, and birth; the rhythms of nature is to live in order. We get to truly live the passage in Ecclesiastes: a time to sow, a time to reap, a time to build up, a time to tear down (Eccl. 3:2–3). There is order in the agrarian lifestyle, in the march of the sun across the sky, and in the seasons across the calendar. God is the author of such order. As part of this, I also have had the good fortune to have raised multiple generations of quality horses, which, in turn, means I have had the unique opportunity to be on horseback in a pasture, gathering cattle, realizing that I had ridden five of this horse's brothers, his mother, and his grandmother in the same pasture.

I get to see the order of humanity come in my children and my grandchildren, in their affinity for the land and the livestock. Together, we see the order that is worship, thanksgiving, right use of faculties—and we see its absence in the disorder of our world.

On another front, I've had the good fortune to assist Fr. Chad Ripperger for the last fifteen years in the ministry of healing, liberation, and exorcism. His influence on our family has stretched through the generations. The first Mass served by my grandsons, who had been formed and instructed by my son (their father), was the Traditional Latin Mass for Fr. Ripperger. He has been a good friend and an important part of my family for many years. My experience in investigating cases of extraordinary diabolical activity, including possession cases, has been extensive, as I have sat in solemn session with Fr. Ripperger and several other exorcists over the last twenty-five years. In these sessions, I have seen the results of disorder, the results of sin that opens the soul to a relationship with the diabolical.

All justice must flow vertically before it flows horizontally. The priest in the Traditional Latin Mass will make that Sign of the Cross over fifty times in the course of one Mass. What we say means something, and what we do means more. The army of Clovis, king of the Franks, was converted by seeing their warrior king, hero, and role model genuflect in reverence to the image of our Lord. A boy will likewise be converted by witnessing his own father's act of homage and veneration to our Lord and Savior and Sovereign King, Jesus Christ. As husbands and fathers, we owe it to our families to do what we can to provide them with the Traditional Latin Mass for the generations to come. We need this order. And they need this order.

CHAPTER 14

FR. CRAIG FRIEDLEY

I AM FR. CRAIG Friedley, the pastor at Our Lady of Guadalupe Parish in Queen Creek, Arizona. I was born a cradle Catholic in Chicago. I entered the U.S. Air Force in 1981 and became a fighter pilot (F-111 and F-16). In 2000, I entered Mount Angel Seminary, and in 2007, I was ordained a Catholic priest for the Diocese of Phoenix. In 2014, I became a member of the Arizona Army National Guard to serve as a chaplain. I retired from the military in 2021.

As a child, I remember going to Mass with my father and my older sister. We attended the TLM in Chicago. It was my father who instilled in me the beginnings of my faith to Jesus. My sister and I had to look our best when we went to Mass. I even had a hat that I got to wear while we walked to church on Sunday mornings. It was great; I even got to wear a feather in that hat. It is amazing how small things can make a child happy. My father wanted me to know God personally.

When Mass was going on, we were taught about the reverence, about what was happening. We were taught about the sacred silence that occurs. We were taught about the bells and the words that we were hearing. All of it led to God and to two children who were with their father, learning how to worship God.

I never lost that desire to be close to God. Like many others, I struggled with my faith, especially from high school and into the beginning of my military career. But there was always something about wanting to do things the right way in my life. Something about wanting to follow the "rules of life," which were always intriguing to me. I am somewhat of a perfectionist and a rebel. That may seem to be an oxymoron to others. And yet that is what led me to becoming a priest who celebrates the TLM today.

I am attracted to following the rules and living them. I am attracted to the reason behind the rules that we have. There is not a business or an organization in this world that does not have rules and policies for its members to follow. That was one of the reasons that the military was so attractive to me.

I fell in love with fighter jets at a young age. The precision flying that I got to see at air shows meant that the pilots were doing exactly what they needed to do according to the rules. If those rules were not followed, then a disaster would happen. We have all seen it. We have seen when a rule or guideline is not followed that is meant to be followed—bad things happen; sometimes they can be deadly.

The military pilot is constantly seeking perfection in skill. There are standards that are followed, and the pilot is not only expected to know them; he or she is expected to follow them. They are evaluated every year, and sometimes even more often than that. That is not a problem for pilots; they know the standards, and they live by them. These standards do not cause a sense of panic or uncertainty in a pilot. They provide a set of conditions under which every pilot is competing against every other pilot on an equal basis. That brings about a sense of peace that is both challenging and rewarding.

But what does all this have to do with the TLM? For me, my real interest in the TLM began when I was challenged to do Mass *ad orientem*. I did not even know that that was a thing.

However, I knew that there was something in my Catholic Faith referring to "facing east." As I started to dig into what this was, I was pleasantly surprised at all the symbolism that was involved. When I looked back at some of the courses I took in seminary, especially regarding art and environment, I realized why I was asked to take those courses. Bishop Robert Barron wrote a book, *Heaven in Stone and Glass.* As I read this, I realized that something the Church has been doing for almost two thousand years should not be discounted easily.

I eventually found myself challenged by Bishop Olmsted, as he asked me to become pastor at Our Lady of Guadalupe in Queen Creek, Arizona. Two things hit me right away. The church is *ad orientem* in its facing, and there is a larger-than-life crucifix on the wall above the tabernacle. This may not mean much to some people, but it meant a lot to me the very first time I celebrated a Mass *ad orientem.*

I spent the time and practiced learning what I needed to do facing east, *ad orientem*, while doing the NOM. I was surprised that I had not looked closely at the rules, the standards that are written in the Roman Missal I had been using at every Mass. It is right there in the book. It assumes that the priest is already doing the NOM *ad orientem* to begin with. Even an old dog can learn a new trick! I am not that old yet, but still being in the military as a chaplain, I knew that I had to explore further what this meant to me.

I did my first Mass facing east (as some would say, my back was to the people). I was doing it the best I could without the training I wish I had received in the seminary. That was okay. It went well. I had to make a few corrections as time passed, but I still do it at my parish.

The point that hit me between the eyes, driving home that I needed to do this, was the Consecration at that very first Mass. When I lifted up the Body of Christ above the altar, right in front of my face was the tabernacle and the larger-than-life crucifix. I had tears in my eyes because of the beauty and sacredness of that very moment, where I was in the place of Christ.

Then, just a moment later, I went even deeper into my ontological being as a Catholic priest and pastor of a parish. I then consecrated the wine into the Blood of Christ. I raised the chalice while once again seeing the tabernacle and the crucifix. But this time I saw, for the first time in my life, in the reflection of my chalice, myself and the rest of my parishioners. I realized at that moment my role as a pastor, in the place of Christ, in a way that will never leave me. Once again, the tears of joy in my eyes were exactly what God wanted me to see that day at that Mass.

What happened at that Mass was something that moved me later on to look at the TLM. And I was once again challenged by some parishioners to look into the Latin Mass. I was at first overwhelmed by the challenge. I knew no Latin except for what phrases I have heard and used over the years, like anyone else who attends the NOM.

The first thing I wanted to do was to look into what was involved. I found that something was missing from my formation training as a seminarian. I was neither told this nor advised to address it before becoming a priest in the Diocese of Phoenix. Something was missing from my time in seminary. I had taken elective training in Greek. Hebrew was offered, but I did not do anything with it as a student. But, when it came to Latin, nothing was even offered at my seminary. Here is what it says in canon law, which our Church produces regarding the laws and standards of the Catholic Church: "The program of priestly formation is to provide that students not only are carefully taught their native language but also *understand Latin well* and have a suitable understanding of those foreign languages which seem necessary or useful for their formation or for the exercise of pastoral ministry" (can. 249, emphasis added).

That was a shock to me. To this day I do not "understand Latin well," but I am getting better at it. I appreciated the effort I was able to put into the Greek language. But now I had to start looking at Latin. So my parishioners really had no idea how challenging this would be for me.

As providence would have it for me, when COVID-19 hit our country and the world, I wound up being called to active duty in the Arizona Army National Guard. I had a lot of traveling to do around the state of Arizona. This is a big state by area, really big when it comes to driving around a lot. I found that I had time to dig into Latin and into celebrating the TLM. I loved it and I loved the challenge. Just as with any pilot given a challenging mission, being challenged as a priest to celebrate the TLM was perfect for me.

I had to learn to pronounce Latin beyond what I had heard in the NOM. I was fortunate to have the Priestly Fraternity of St. Peter (F.S.S.P.) right in Phoenix. I spent hours with their priests just going over the Missal. Pronouncing the words, asking questions, practicing the movements, reading the Ordo, looking at the differences and similarities to the Novus Ordo. I eventually got the opportunity to go to the F.S.S.P. seminary in Nebraska, and I attended the practicum of the TLM. That was the icing on the cake for me. I knew I could do this.

What my parishioners did not know was that it would take me a year to do all of this, just like it took me a year to first learn how to fly jets in the military. My learning has not stopped, and it will not stop. I keep improving and learning from my mistakes. What I do know is that the TLM helped me to become a man who loves the Mass and all the intricacies of it.

I am delving deeply into the reasons why things are done the way they are in the TLM. The rules and standards that I learned to love as a pilot translated perfectly into learning, living, and loving the TLM. A priest is not his own. The TLM recognizes that and helps each priest who celebrates this Mass to step into the role in the place of Christ.

It is never about the individual priest, his wants and desires, his particular way of doing a Mass, his opinions, or anything about his personality that belongs to the Mass. Worship and celebration of the TLM allows every individual to participate in a way that acknowledges that the Mass is all about Christ. When every priest is doing it the same way, the proper way, this is attractive to any man who desires to follow Jesus. The standards of the military were just a preliminary warm-up for a young man serving his country to become a priest serving his God — serving his God and parish.

A priest following Jesus is a man of God. For me, learning and doing the TLM reaffirms my role as a man of God doing what he is called to do. The TLM is not just for the priest; it is also for any man to become a man of God, one who is willing to set aside the things of this world and help bring about the Kingdom of God here on earth every time the sacred Mass is offered.

CHAPTER 15

BAS RUTTEN

MY NAME IS BAS Rutten, and I am a retired mixed martial artist. In 1997, I emigrated from the Netherlands to America to live the American dream, and I am currently doing exactly that. I love this country, but we need to get it stronger.

We Catholics aren't supposed to brag, but here goes: I hold three world titles in Japan for an organization named Pancrase, and then in 1999 I became the first European fighter to be crowned a UFC champion. I didn't lose any of my last twenty-two fights, have an almost 90 percent finishing rate, and still hold, to this day, the highest striking accuracy in the entire MMA world. I am also in the 2015 class of the UFC Hall of Fame. Needless to say, I always considered myself a "tough guy."

That is, until I got back to the Faith in 2014.

You see, I always thought that "doing whatever you want to do" was being the man, that it was giving me "freedom." Doing things like drinking, overeating, drugs, being with women, fighting, anger, gossiping, judging—you name it. But as I got deeper into the Faith, I realized it was all the opposite of being a tough guy. I had nothing under control. I couldn't stop, just to name a few, drinking, doing drugs, being angry, judging, shouting stupid stuff, heck, even using a lot of profanity. I realized that all these habits and behaviors were controlling *me*, that those vices were simply telling *me* what I needed to do — and then I, being a slave to them, did exactly that.

But, being the fierce competitor that I am, I just saw this as my next and final fight in life. I want to be in control of my life and keep that up till the end so I have a chance to go to Heaven, but I also know and understand that this is very hard to achieve. *Challenge accepted!*

I speak at Catholic events, and I talk about what kind of man I want to be, and when I give this next line coming up, I always get asked to repeat it a few times because people want to write it down.

So, what kind of man do I want to be?

I want to be a man who can overcome his weaknesses, vices, and imperfections. A man who is not a slave to his passions, emotions, and desires, but a real man, who is in control of himself.

Once I heard that line, I felt an urgent need to become exactly that man, but again, it's very hard to achieve, especially in this weak society we live in right now. When we even have the pope saying that he wants to demasculinize the Church, that's really bad. To me, it feels like the pope doesn't want us to follow the greatest person who ever lived (and is still with us): Jesus Christ. Apparently, Jesus didn't say, "If any man would come after me, let him deny himself and take up his cross and follow me" (Matt. 16:24).

What does that mean "deny himself and take up his cross?" That means we have to deny all the vices out there — we have to stop being a PUSI! Yes, that word sounds like what many people believe I am saying, but it's not *that* word. It's an abbreviation of the word *pusillanimous*, which means "lack of courage and determination, or even cowardly." Unfortunately, we live in a world where many are becoming that person. We are becoming *weak*. Nothing can be a struggle anymore. We are being taught that "you are good the way you are," even when you are not. When you try to avoid stress and difficult situations, you will *never* get stronger. The only way to get rid of problems is to attack that problem so it's not a problem anymore. We need to fight, fight for ourselves to become the person God truly wants us to be: mentally, physically, and especially spiritually.

We are becoming effeminate. "Wow," you might be thinking, "that doesn't sound *manly* at all!" And you are correct. Do you know what *effeminate* means? It's an attachment to pleasure and an unwillingness to suffer. The only way to stop a vice is to say *no* to that vice and then start working on getting stronger and making sure you never give in to that vice again.

You see, nobody likes to be overweight, or drunk, or on drugs, or stuck on whatever vice you have, but the only way to beat it is to say *no*. Now, this is the good part: The more you say *no*, the stronger you get, and the easier it becomes to say no. This is what they call *virtue*.

But the more you give in to weak habits, the weaker you get and the harder it becomes to say no to those habits. Those are called *vices*. Virtue makes you stronger, vice makes you weaker. Start this fight today, not tomorrow or next week. *Today.*

I love the TLM. I was just interviewed for the last part of the *Mass of the Ages* video that came out in March of 2024.[62] They asked me to say what the Latin Mass means to me, and here are the exact words I said on that video:

> When I walk into the Traditional Latin Mass, I instantly feel connected to something greater than myself. Everything about it is transcendent: the Latin, the chanting,

---

[62] This interview was not included in the final edited version of this documentary.

the incense, the silence. All these elements give me a sense of connecting to a distant past. But they also inspire a bond of unity with the present times. I mean, think about it. Every Catholic person across the globe is experiencing the exact same sacrifice in the exact same way. How cool is that? Listen, the Traditional Mass is truly Catholic. It's universal, and it is also manly, sacrificial. Then I've also learned that every movement of the priest is purposeful. I am talking about every hand gesture, each turn, even the position of the priest's eyes, is all meant, in some way, to symbolize and represent the sacrifice of Christ. Another great thing? Everybody is in sync with the responses, and no cell phones will be ringing. The last thing: I love how everybody, including the kids, is nicely dressed. In every aspect, it's simply beautiful! When you attend a Latin Mass, there is no doubt that it is worship as God intends.

So, stop being a PUSI, get your life under control, and I promise you, you are going to feel great, and your family members and friends will enjoy seeing that new person as well. Living healthy — eating healthy food, working out, and having temperance with everything out there — keeps you ready for whatever problems life is going to throw at you and/or your loved ones.

Deo gratias!

CHAPTER 16

DAN SCHNEIDER

As I RECENTLY PULLED into a monastery for a Rorate Mass, I could not help but notice the number of pickup trucks in the parking lot. In the distance, I saw a man kneeling on the gravel before a priest in a cassock who was giving him absolution. Inside the dark church were mostly men, some alone, and some who had brought their young families. The mood was prayerful, solemn, and reverent. Rosary beads dangled from the majority of the men's hands. Cardinal Robert Sarah wrote that "marriage between a man and a woman is also marriage between man and the Church, who is the bride of Christ." Combining their voices with the feminine voices of the Carmelite sisters chanting from behind the grille, the men at this Mass and their families understood this instinctively. The chapel was filled with regular guys, exmilitary and law enforcement, truck drivers, farmers, engineers, and business owners. No one held hands, everyone was respectfully dressed, and everyone knelt to receive Holy Communion. Most knew it was also the final of three Ember Days, so they were fasting. No one felt the need to speak. "If the Church wants to attract men," I thought, "this is a good start."

The combination of the darkness and the cold desert air, combined with the somber tone, stirred up in me memories of Holy Mass in the desert sands of Saudi Arabia and Iraq. I am a former U.S. Army helicopter pilot and cavalry officer. Early each morning, we would perform our preflight at first light, usually in silence, before flying our missions. The preflight checklist always included checking the large nut that held the rotors in place. We called this the "Jesus nut" because if it came loose, the rotors would come off and, well, you would be going to meet Jesus that day. When the brigade Catholic chaplain learned I was Catholic and had gone to Notre Dame, he asked me to fly him each week throughout the area of operation so he could say Holy Mass for small groups of Catholic men so they could meet their Sunday obligation. I hauled him all over the desert each Sunday. The sound of the *wop-wop-wop* of our approach alerted the troopers to pull their Bradley Fighting Vehicles back and form a hasty perimeter before dismounting. Some "went for a walk" with the padre before Mass so he could hear Confessions. Then we all knelt while Father offered Mass. In that faraway desert and before a makeshift altar, despite our being outdoors and surrounded with the smells and sounds of combat, the mood was equally prayerful, solemn, and reverent. These are the marks of the Mass of the Ages—and these are what attract men.

When I came back from Iraq and left the Army, I missed the brotherhood and comradery of the military, but I especially missed the noble simplicity of Holy Mass I had experienced. What I found in the typical parish was quite the opposite—an effeminate and feminized liturgy that focused more on community and social action than an encounter with the Other, the transcendent God. Instead of a going upward to meet the living God, everyone seemed content in bringing God down to us. What was manufactured was a sugary Jesus who demanded nothing of us and offered no challenge to mortify the passions through fasting and penance or to go to Confession and become better men. There was also no talk of being a leader in the home, like we were trained to be on the battlefield. Over time, predictably, many of my Army buddies began leaving the Church.

What is lost today, in all of our talk of a "new evangelization," is that the masculine mind is drawn to the transcendent—to beauty, goodness, and truth—and not emotionalism or religious entertainment. Perhaps this is why the parishes with reverent liturgies are often the ones filled with young families. In *The Spirit of the Liturgy*, Cardinal Joseph Ratzinger (Pope Benedict XVI) warned of the temptation that arises when "people cannot cope with the invisible, remote, and mysterious God." Reflecting on the Golden Calf incident during the desert wanderings of ancient Israel, he warned that when the worshipping community loses the sense of mystery, a subtle danger creeps into its liturgy. "Worship," he stated, "is no longer going up to God, but drawing God down into one's own world." When that happens, our worship "becomes a feast that the community gives itself." When man and not God becomes the focus of our liturgy, we repeat the error of Israel in the desert, creating "a circle closed in on itself: eating, drinking and making merry." Worship becomes self-seeking, or worse, he said, "a dance around the gold calf in a festival of self-affirmation." This is most acutely seen when we applaud some human achievement (birthdays or anniversaries included) at Mass. Applause at Mass, noted Cardinal Ratzinger, is "a sure sign that the essence of liturgy has totally disappeared and been replaced by a kind of religious entertainment." Notably, none of the men clapped at the end of our combat Masses. They prayed silently, climbed back into their Bradleys, and went back to work. Men do not go to church to be entertained or for recreation, but to glorify God by offering true worship, to enter into the mystery of the eternal sacrifice of Calvary.

Men need fraternity, order, and ritual and to be challenged to follow in the footsteps of the Lord. This includes learning and living the fullness of truth, growing in virtue, subduing our lower passions, and becoming holy. Not every man will have the experience of soldiering in physical combat, but all are called to militate and conquer spiritual battles. St. Paul said that in his own spiritual life he is not just "shadowboxing" but fights "so as to win" a crown (1 Cor. 9:24, 26, NABRE). To that end, he wrote to St. Timothy words that apply to every man today: "But as for you, man of God," you need to avoid vice and grow in virtue and "fight the good fight" (1 Tim. 6:11–12). He challenged Timothy further to "bear your share of hardship along with me like a good soldier of Christ Jesus" (2 Tim. 2:3, NABRE). The word for "bear your share of hardship" that St. Paul uses means to suffer with, to co-endure, to bear under. This is what soldiers do. In military terms, this means to gear up and grind it out together—for each other and for a cause greater than oneself. Notably, the word St. Paul uses for *good* (as in a "good" soldier) refers not to physical skills but to the interior disposition of being virtuous, honorable, noble, morally beautiful. This is the call of men today—to win victory over spiritual battles through sacrifice and virtue.

What also attracts men is the clear and unadulterated truth. Perhaps what is most pronounced, and attractive, in the TLM is the sacrificial nature of the ancient liturgy. In fact, it is principally by means of the liturgy that the Church catechizes her children and unveils the mysteries of our redemption. The ancient Greek word *liturgeis* means "a work on behalf of the people" (and the Benedictines still refer to the Divine Office as the *opus Dei*, "the work of God"). Just as soldiers learn from the combat experience of seasoned veterans, we also need to learn from the lessons of the past. In the ancient mind, the word *history* (Greek *historein*) was understood differently than the mere categorizing of events and people of the past, as it means now in the popular and modern usage of the term. For the ancients, *history* meant either (1) *to investigate* and inquire into the meaning of past events or (2) *to remember* the great deeds of the heroes of our past so that they and the lessons from their lives are not forgotten. In that sense, then, liturgy is a work of history in that it recalls and makes present the mystery of salvation. At the first Holy Mass (where two sacraments were instituted, the Eucharist and Holy Orders), Jesus commanded His apostles to "do this in remembrance of me" (Luke 22:19). As Dom Gaspar Lefebvre, O.S.B., reminds us in the *Saint Andrew Missal*, "The Church reproduces in her liturgy all phases of the life of her Divine Founder." Whether in a combat outpost, a quiet monastery, or the noblest of cathedrals, the Holy Mass perpetuates the most important fact of human history, namely, both recalling and making present, in an unbloody way, the sacrifice of Jesus Christ on Calvary. The feasts and fasts, solemnities and octaves, rites and Masses (like the Rorate Mass) all become a living canvas upon which God draws us into the stream of salvation history.

If we forget the heroes of our past, the saints who battled and defeated Satan in their flesh by means of the ancient weapons of tradition, we are doomed to repeat the mistakes of the past. The great saints who defeated the enemy through heroic virtue tapped into the wellspring of divine worship and learned to be "a good soldier of Jesus Christ" by uniting their suffering to His. A phrase attributed to St. Bernard of Chartres describes what the force of a living tradition can bring to bear to the modern world: "We are dwarfs, sitting on the shoulders of giants." Without the help of those who have gone before us, we will never discover the truths needed for today, for the battle that lies ahead. Military tacticians know this instinctively. They adapt their strategies to a shifting battle plain, while never forgetting that the basics of combat never change. To attract more men, the

modern Church needs to recapture the sacrificial spirit of soldiering for Christ and the rich theological patrimony experienced
in the prayerfulness, solemnity, and reverence of her ancient
liturgy.

CHAPTER 17

Scott Sullivan

IF YOU ARE LIKE most men, at least the ones in my social circle, you may be turned off by many of the modern forms of Catholic liturgy. Many men have noticed that these modern forms seem very feminine in tone, appealing to the emotions through sappy songs that sound like they were written in the '70s. Unfortunately, in my experience, these feminine forms of liturgy have caused many men to feel not at home in church. Churches are seen as women's clubs. As a result, men don't want to go.

But it seems to me that it shouldn't be this way. In a world where masculinity is often associated with strength, discipline, and a sense of purpose, the TLM holds a unique appeal for men seeking a deeper connection to their spirituality. As a former kickboxer, I have discovered that this ancient liturgy, conducted in Latin, embodies qualities that resonate deeply with the masculine spirit. In the following paragraphs, I will delve into the reasons why the TLM seems particularly appealing to men.

The Power of Mystery

Men appreciate depth. One of the most captivating aspects of the TLM is its air of mystery. Conducted in a language that may be unfamiliar to many, it creates a sense of awe and reverence. This mysterious quality can be especially appealing to men, who often appreciate the allure of the unknown. The TLM invites men to engage their curiosity, encouraging them to explore the depths of their faith and find spiritual fulfillment in the midst of mystery.

The Engagement of the Intellect

Men tend to be more intellectual and less emotional. Liturgies based on triggering emotions can, then, be a sort of turnoff for men. In my experience, the traditional liturgies are built upon the intellectual tradition of the Church. This is especially true of the homilies that are typically heard at the traditional liturgy. The doctrines discussed run deep, engaging the intellect and having more of an appeal to men.

The Strength of Tradition

The TLM is steeped in centuries of tradition, which adds to its appeal for men seeking a connection to their roots. The use of Latin, a language with a rich history, creates a sense of continuity with the past. Men are drawn to the strength and stability that tradition provides, as it offers a solid foundation upon which to build their faith. The rituals and symbols of the Latin Mass evoke a sense of order and discipline, mirroring the values that many men hold dear.

The Importance of Reverence

Reverence is a cornerstone of the TLM, and it resonates deeply with the masculine spirit. The precise movements of the priest, the use of incense, and the solemnity of the liturgy all contribute to an atmosphere of reverence and respect. The TLM is God centered, not centered on us. Men appreciate the opportunity to approach their faith with a sense of solemnity, as it allows them to express their devotion in a way that aligns with their natural inclination for reverence.

The Call to Sacrifice

Modern psychology says, "I'm okay, and you're okay." This is not the message of traditional Catholicism. The TLM emphasizes the importance of sacrifice, a concept that holds great significance for men. Just as a kickboxer must make sacrifices in training and competition, the TLM calls men to offer themselves in service to a higher purpose. It reminds men of the value of self-sacrifice, encouraging them to lay aside their own desires and ambitions for the greater good. This call to sacrifice resonates deeply with the masculine spirit. By nature, men can be prone to sacrifice themselves for the common good.

Regimen and Order

The TLM is a ritual steeped in tradition and order. From the moment you step into the church, you are enveloped in an atmosphere of reverence and solemnity. The precise movements of the priest, the carefully chosen words, and the rich symbolism all contribute to a sense of purpose and discipline that resonates deeply with me. The process is militaristic in a sense.

In many ways, the TLM reminds me of the training I underwent as a kickboxer. Just as I would spend hours perfecting my technique and honing my skills, the priest and the congregation invest time and effort into preparing for the Mass. The attention to detail, the focus on proper form, and the commitment to excellence all mirror the dedication required to excel in any physical discipline.

Introspection over Outward Expression

Finally, the TLM offers a space for introspection and self-reflection. There is not this push to interact with other members of the congregation during Mass. The invitation is internal. As I participate in the liturgy, I am reminded of the importance of humility, self-control, and self-sacrifice. These virtues are not exclusive to any gender, but they certainly resonate with the ideals of masculinity that I have come to appreciate.

In conclusion, it seems to me that the TLM holds a special allure for men seeking a deeper connection to their spirituality. Its mysterious nature, rooted in centuries of tradition, creates an atmosphere of reverence and respect. The TLM invites men to explore the depths of their faith, embracing the call to sacrifice and finding strength in the rituals and symbols of the liturgy. By engaging in the TLM, men can tap into their masculinity in a way that aligns with their values and provides a profound sense of fulfillment in their spiritual journey.

APPENDICES

REFLECTIONS ON THE PASSION IN THE ACTIONS OF THE TLM

A Pious Reflection on the Latin Mass, Which the Faithful May Use to Derive Spiritual Fruit.[63]

THE PRIEST AT MASS	CHRIST
1 Enters the Sanctuary	Enters the Garden of Olives
2 Begins prayers at the foot of the Altar	Begins prayer in the garden
3 Says the *Confiteor* ("I Confess")	Falls down in agony, sweats blood
4 Goes to the Epistle side of the Altar	Is bound and as a prisoner is led to Annas
5 Reads the Introit	Is falsely accused by Annas and blasphemed
6 Goes to the middle of the Altar, recites *Kyrie Eleison*	Is brought to Caiaphas; Is denied 3x by Peter
7 Turns to the people and says "Dominus vobiscum"	Looks at Peter and converts him
8 Goes to the Roman Missal and reads the Collect and Epistle	Is brought to Pilate
9 Goes to the middle of the Altar, then to the Gospel side	Is taken to Herod and mocked
10 Returns to the middle of the Altar	Is led back to Pilate

[63] "The Holy Sacrifice of the Mass Is … Christ's Passion and Death on Calvary." The Fatima Center. https://fatima.org/wp-content/uploads/2019/05/LF412-Mass-Explained-Web.pdf. Last accessed July 2, 2024.

OFFERTORY

11 Uncovers the chalice	Is stripped of His garments
12 Offers the bread and wine	Is scourged at the pillar
13 Covers the chalice with the pall	Is crowned with thorns
14 Washes his hands at the Epistle side of the Altar	Is declared innocent by Pilate
15 Turns to the people and says "Orate Fratres …" ("Pray brethren…")	Is shown to the people by Pilate who says "Ecce Homo" ("Behold the man")
16 Prays in a low voice, the Secret (prayer)	Is mocked and spat upon
17 Recites the Preface and Sanctus—bell is rung	Christ is condemned; Barabbas is freed

CANON OF THE MASS

18 Makes the Commemoration of the living	Carries the Cross to Calvary
19 Blesses the bread and wine with the sign of the cross 5x	Is nailed to the Cross

CONSECRATION

20 Consecrates the Host, adores and elevates It	Christ is raised on the Cross
21 Consecrates the wine and elevates the chalice	Blood of Christ flows from His wounds
22 Prays in a low voice	Hangs on the Cross; sees His Mother kneeling
23 Says aloud, "Nobis quoque peccatoribus"	Prays for all mankind
24 Recites aloud the *Pater Noster* ("Our Father")	Speaks the seven last words on the Cross
25 Breaks the Sacred Host	Dies on the Cross
26 Drops a particle of the Host into the chalice	Christ's soul descends into Limbo
27 Recites the Agnus Dei ("Lamb of God")	Christ is acknowledged to be the Son of God by those standing beneath the Cross

COMMUNION

28 Receives the Body and Blood of Christ — Christ's body is laid in the sepulcher

29 Cleanes the chalice — Christ's body is anointed in the sepulcher

30 Prepares the chalice on the Altar again — Rises from the dead

31 Turns to the people and says "Dominus vobiscum" — Appears to His Mother and Disciples

32 Reads Communion and Post Communion prayers — Teaches for forty days

33 Turns to the people and says the last "Dominus vobiscum" — Bids farewell to His Disciples

34 Says the "Ite Missa est" — Commissions the Apostles to preach the Gospel to all nations; ascends into Heaven

35 Gives the blessing to the people — Sends down the Holy Ghost on Pentecost

36 Reads the last Gospel. — Is preached and worshiped throughout the world as the Son of God made Man

ABUSES IN THE NOM: SUGGESTIONS FOR FURTHER READING

Bukuras, Joe, Shannon Mullen, and Carl Bunderson, "Indigenous Prayers, Dancing in San Bernardino Synod Mass Spark Backlash: Did an Aztec Demon Appear at the End of Mass?," *Catholic News Agency*, October 25, 2021.

ChurchPOP Editors, "Irish Priest Rides Scooter for Christmas Eve Mass Recessional in Viral Video," ChurchPOP, December 26, 2019.

"Father Guilherme Plays as DJ to Wake Up the People (JMJ — Pope Francis in Portugal — 2023)," Jorge Rosa, August 6, 2023, YouTube video, https://www.youtube.com/watch?v=T5tAp6bZZhg.

Firer, Alex, "Catholic Church Flies Blessed Sacrament from Drone," *What's Trending*, April 4, 2018.

"A Foretaste of Amazon: Demonic Masks Appear during Bishops' Mass," Gloria.tv, September 3, 2019.

"Gay Priest at Italian Wedding," Jump Box, July 17, 2013, YouTube video, https://www.youtube.com/watch?v=pOkFd2p08NU.

"Italy: Little Girl Distributes Communion at Novus Ordo Mass!," Novus Ordo Watch, October 25, 2023.

"Priest Raps at Mass and Organizes Whiskey Retreats," Catholic Conclave, March 7, 2023.

"The Real Nacho Libre: The Unbelievable Life of Fray Tormenta," *Tú Decides/You Decide*, December 9, 2015.

Tondo, Lorenzo, "Italian Priest Uses Inflatable Mattress as Altar during Mass in Sea," Complicit Clergy, July 30, 2022.

PRACTICES OF EUCHARISTIC DEVOTION IN THE MASS[64]

Practice	Traditional	New
The faithful receiving kneeling and on the tongue	Required	Optional
The faithful receiving from the hands of a priest/deacon	Required	Optional
The faithful receiving with a Communion paten	Required	Optional
The minister of Communion making the sign of the cross with the host over the Communicant	Required	Suppressed
The priest keeping his thumb and forefinger joined from Consecration to ablutions	Required	Optional
The priest genuflecting before and after any handling of the Sacred Species	Required	Suppressed
The priest genuflecting before and after each elevation at the Consecration	Required	Reduced to one genuflection
Laypeople forbidden from touching the Sacred Species	Required	Suppressed

[64] Fr. John Zuhlsdorf, "If the Eucharistic Revival Doesn't Address These ...," *Fr. Z's Blog*, November 18, 2022. Eucharistic revival is particularly suited to happen only in the TLM. https://wdtprs.com/2022/11/if-the-eucharistic-revival-doesnt-address-these/

Practice	Traditional	New
Laypeople forbidden from touching the sacred vessels	Required	Suppressed
The priest not turning his back on the tabernacle for more than a passing moment	Required	Optional
Fingers purified with wine and water	Required	Suppressed
Sacred vessels purified with wine and water	Required	Optional
Purification at the altar	Required	Optional
Purification during Mass	Required	Optional
Clergy genuflecting to the tabernacle during the Mass proper	Required	Suppressed

About the Author

Jesse Romero is a full-time bilingual Catholic lay evangelist who is nationally recognized for his dynamic Christ-centered preaching. He is a retired Los Angeles deputy sheriff, three-time world police boxing champion, and a two-time USA kickboxing champion. Jesse makes the sometimes complex teachings of the Faith understandable with his straight-talk approach. He has a degree from Mount St. Mary's College in Los Angeles and an M.A. in Catholic theology from Franciscan University in Ohio. Recipient of the Archbishop Fulton Sheen Award in 2010 and the Defender of the Faith Award in 2014, Jesse was inducted into the Catholic Sports Hall of Fame in 2015. He hosts two radio podcasts daily on *Virgin Most Powerful Radio*.

Sophia Institute

Sᴏᴘʜɪᴀ Iɴsᴛɪᴛᴜᴛᴇ ɪs ᴀ nonprofit institution that seeks to nurture the spiritual, moral, and cultural life of souls and to spread the gospel of Christ in conformity with the authentic teachings of the Roman Catholic Church.

Sophia Institute Press fulfills this mission by offering translations, reprints, and new publications that afford readers a rich source of the enduring wisdom of mankind.

Sophia Institute also operates the popular online resource CatholicExchange.com. *Catholic Exchange* provides world news from a Catholic perspective as well as daily devotionals and articles that will help readers to grow in holiness and live a life consistent with the teachings of the Church.

In 2013, Sophia Institute launched Sophia Institute for Teachers to renew and rebuild Catholic culture through service to Catholic education. With the goal of nurturing the spiritual, moral, and cultural life of souls, and an abiding respect for the role and work of teachers, we strive to provide materials and programs that are at once enlightening to the mind and ennobling to the heart; faithful and complete, as well as useful and practical.

Sophia Institute gratefully recognizes the Solidarity Association for preserving and encouraging the growth of our apostolate over the course of many years. Without their generous and timely support, this book would not be in your hands.

www.SophiaInstitute.com
www.CatholicExchange.com
www.SophiaTeachers.org

Sophia Institute Press is a registered trademark of Sophia Institute.
Sophia Institute is a tax-exempt institution as defined by the
Internal Revenue Code, Section 501(c)(3). Tax ID 22-2548708.